English for NSW YEAR 10

– STAGE 5 –

Emma Wynne-Jones
Bronwyn Ralphs

First published in 2024

Insight Publications Pty Ltd
3/350 Charman Road
Cheltenham Victoria 3192
Australia

Tel: +61 3 8571 4950
Fax: +61 3 8571 0257
Email: books@insightpublications.com.au

www.insightpublications.com.au

English for NSW, Year 10, Stage 5 / Emma Wynne-Jones, Bronwyn Ralphs

ISBN:

9781923016507

Edited by Kathryn Tafra
Cover by Melisa Paredes
Proofread by Lisa Neale
Internal design by Federico Fonseca
Typesetting by Melisa Paredes
Printed by Markono Print Media Pte Ltd

CONTENTS

CONTENTS

UNIT 01

Writing worlds – a study of the novel

Unit inquiry question:
How does the novel explore the human condition?

Students will analyse the stylistic features of novels and examine how they can shape and be shaped by its purpose. Through this, students will consider the different ways we give significance and worth to a text.

As they grow their understanding of and respond to the novel, students will examine point of view, characterisation and narrative conventions, and experiment with these in their own creative compositions.

Students will also have the opportunity to reflect on how their appreciation of the novel has been enhanced though the process of re-reading and re-examining different examples of the novel form.

This unit has been broken into three chapters, which each look at a different aspect of texts and the world and raise additional inquiry questions.

CHAPTER 1

Soaring to survival – *Lark*

Lark tells the endearing story of two brothers and how their faith in one another is put to the test as one lies injured in a snowstorm. This chapter focuses on storytelling through the creation of convincing settings and characters.

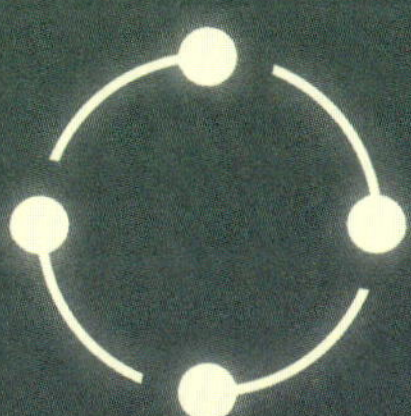

CHAPTER 2

Finding your voice – *Catching Teller Crow*

The multiple narrative novel *Catching Teller Crow* tells a compelling tale of loss, love and life while exploring experiences of First Nations people.

CHAPTER 3

It was sort of funny, in a way – *The Catcher in the Rye*

An exploration of the Bildungsroman genre through a study of *The Catcher in the Rye*, its characters and its themes.

The learning activities within each chapter and the summative assessment options (on pages 39–41) provide opportunities to assess student achievement of the following outcomes.

Outcome and focus area	Content point
EN5-RVL-01 **Reading, viewing and listening to texts**	**Reading, viewing and listening skills**
	Apply reading pathways appropriate to form, purpose and meaning, and connect ideas within and between texts
	Use contextual cues to infer the meaning of unfamiliar or complex words
	Develop a deeper understanding of themes, ideas or attitudes by revisiting and reinterpreting texts to find new meaning
	Reading, viewing and listening for meaning
	Analyse how the use of language forms and features in texts have the capacity to create multiple meanings
	Analyse the main ideas and thematic concerns represented in texts
	Investigate how layers of meaning are constructed in texts and how this shapes a reader's understanding and engagement
	Reflecting
	Reflect on how an appreciation of texts can be enhanced through re-reading, and close or critical study
EN5-URA-01 **Understanding and responding to texts A**	**Connotation, imagery and symbol**
	Analyse how Aboriginal and Torres Strait Islander authors use figurative language and devices to represent culture, identity and experience
	Point of view
	Examine elements of focalisation, such as omniscience, limitations, indirect speech, tone, reliability and multiple narrators, and how these interact to shape perceptions of meaning in texts, and apply this in own texts
	Recognise the difference between the actual author and authorial voice in texts and use this understanding to create texts with other kinds of imagined authors
	Characterisation
	Explore how characters in texts can be lifelike constructions with whom audiences establish intellectual and emotional connections, and can be perceived to reflect, challenge or subvert particular values and attitudes
	Narrative
	Analyse how narrative conventions vary across genres, modes, media and contexts, and how they can be used to represent ideas and values and shape responses, and apply this understanding in own texts

EN5-URB-01 **Understanding and responding to texts B**	**Argument and authority**
	Analyse how an engaging personal voice in texts can represent a perspective or argument and communicate a sense of authority, and experiment with these ideas in own texts
	Theme
	Analyse how themes can be understood to underpin cohesive meaning in texts, and apply this understanding in own texts
	Appreciate the role of the audience in perceiving themes and how these themes can offer insights into an author's perspective
	Style
	Analyse how the distinctive aesthetic qualities and stylistic features of a text can shape and be shaped by its purpose, and experiment with this in own texts
EN5-URC-01 **Understanding and responding to texts C**	**Genre**
	Analyse how elements of genre in texts can shape the way ideas and values are represented and perceived, and experiment with elements of genre in own texts to shape meaning and response
	Literary value
	Analyse and evaluate how thematic and aesthetic qualities of a text contribute to the different ways an audience questions and negotiates the value of the text in particular contexts
EN5-ECA-01 **Expressing ideas and composing texts A**	**Writing**
	Experiment with language to create tone, atmosphere and mood
	Use tense accurately and purposefully
	Apply narrative voice to depict complex ideas and enhance engagement
	Sentence-level grammar and punctuation
	Select and justify the use of varied sentence type, length and complexity to support cohesion and for effect
EN5-ECB-01 **Expressing ideas and composing texts B**	**Planning, monitoring and revising**
	Engage with model texts to develop and refine features, structures and stylistic approaches in own work
	Reflecting
	Reflect on own texts, using technical vocabulary to explain and evaluate authorial decisions appropriate to the target audience and specific purpose

CHAPTER 1: SOARING TO SURVIVAL – *LARK*

Chapter overview

In this chapter, you will learn about the importance of realistic settings, characters and themes in underpinning the meaning of a narrative.

You will explore the ways in which characters' motivations and relationships engage the audience through their lifelike experiences, and how they can reflect and challenge some values and attitudes.

Success criteria: In this chapter, I will be successful when I can ...

- connect with a model text to develop and refine features, structures and stylistic approaches in my writing
- recognise that characters and settings can be lifelike representations designed to appeal to the reader
- write an engaging opening to a narrative.

Chapter inquiry questions

- What's in a title?
- Are beginnings crucial to engage the reader?
- In what ways can setting and atmosphere engage the audience?
- How can a single symbol enhance the narrative?

Key vocabulary

- Prediction
- Hook
- In medias res

What's in a title?

The front cover, blurb and title of a novel often determine how far a reader delves into the pages, if they delve at all.

The title of the novel is often a clue to the content – sometimes in an obvious way but often more enigmatically. This is to stir the interest and imagination of the reader.

1.1.1 Warm-up

Lark by Anthony McGowan is the last in *The Truth of Things* quartet.

VOCABULARY

Brock
noun: an old-fashioned word for a badger, a large black and white animal that is nocturnal and lives in a burrow underground

Pike
noun: a type of fish, long like an eel but not as skinny

Rook
noun: a type of bird, big and black

Lark
noun: a small, brown bird that is known for its beautiful singing

1 Go online and find the book covers of the four novels, *Brock*, *Pike*, *Rook* and *Lark*. Identify similarities and differences between *Lark* and the other three.

Similarities	Differences

Try accessing a summary of the novel. You can find a written review via the QR code.

Are beginnings crucial to engage the reader?

Novels can begin in a myriad of ways. They can begin with:

- **describing a place**, orientating the story in a particular time, season or setting or by offering a clear **impression of a central character** either through a unique narrative style or detailed observations
- an unusual opening or telling of an **unexpected plot action** – like a car chase or falling from a rooftop
- **an image or symbol** that is going to be central to the story in some way
- a short sentence or question for the reader (that should always avoid clichés)
- **dialogue**, as if the reader has entered a conversation halfway through. This technique is known as opening '**in medias res**', which is Latin for 'in the midst of the action'. This can often be an effective way to grab the immediate attention of the reader.
- **the end** – this can reflect the narrator's thoughts after the events of the story have already finished.

Whatever the technique, the opening is designed to capture the reader from the outset by shocking or intriguing them or making them laugh. Ultimately the writer wants to 'hook' the reader into reading beyond the first page.

1.1.2 Understanding and responding to texts A

This is how *Lark* begins:

> 'I don't bloody like it.'
>
> 'Language, Kenny,' I said to my brother. 'You don't have to bloody well say bloody all the bloody time. It's not clever, and it's not funny.'
>
> I copied the whining voice of Mr Kimble, our English teacher. But it was wasted on Kenny as he didn't go to my school.
>
> 'But it's bloody cold,' Kenny said.
>
> 'I know.'
>
> 'And we're bloody lost.'
>
> 'I bloody know.'

1 Which opening technique do you think McGowan decided to use here? Why is it effective?

____

____

____

2 Why do you think the writer repeats the word 'bloody' so many times? Do you think this engages the reader or not? Justify your thinking.

3 After reading this opening what does the reader now know about the characters in this story?

After this exchange between Kenny and his younger brother Nicky, the author uses the convention of setting to orientate the reader in time and place.

> I looked around. It had stopped snowing, but the path had almost vanished. I saw white fields and stone walls. The black skeletons of trees climbing out of the frozen earth. The sky was a sort of pale grey, like a seagull's back. In fact, the sky was the weirdest thing about it all. You couldn't see any clouds, or any of the blue in between the clouds. Just this solid grey nothing like cold porridge, going on for ever.
>
> I had Tina, our Jack Russell, on the lead. She'd enjoyed the snow to begin with, snapping at it and chewing mouthfuls, as if she'd caught a rat. But now she looked as fed up as us. She was getting on a bit, and the cold had got into her bones.

4 What figurative device is used in the line 'The black skeletons of trees climbing out of the frozen earth' and why is this an effective image?

1.1.3 Expressing ideas and composing texts A

You have read the opening lines of the novel *Lark* and considered some ways in which McGowan tries to 'hook' his reader.

Your goal: To engage with the model text (the opening of *Lark*) to develop and refine features, structures and stylistic approaches in your own writing by:

- experimenting with language to establish either setting or character
- using tense accurately and with intention
- making sure you vary your sentence styles and lengths
- employing a clear narrative voice.

Your task: In your English notebook write two openings to two different narratives. In each, use a different style of beginning chosen from those mentioned previously to craft your first paragraph/s to engage or 'hook' your reader.

[Clue: sometimes it helps to have a reader in your mind. McGowan has said that the reader in his mind for writing *Lark* was male, from the North of England and not from a background of privilege.]

1.1.4 Expressing ideas and composing texts B

In pairs, read each other's story starters. Offer feedback based on the success criteria above and on what you have learned so far about novel openings.

Then, in response to that feedback and your own thinking, reflect on your writing.

Decide which of your paragraphs is the best and use technical vocabulary to explain and evaluate your authorial choices. You might want to include who your target audience is and how this novel opening is specifically engaging for them.

Write a short reflection.

In what ways can setting and atmosphere engage the audience?

A realistic setting enhances the audience's enjoyment. If the reader can visualise where the story's action takes place, even if they have never been there, they can better imagine the characters' interactions and the atmosphere such a setting creates.

Attention to detail and figurative language choices can really make a difference in creating a sense of place and building atmosphere.

Scan the QR code to access additional activities.

Catching up with the story ...

When Nicky is lying badly injured and in extreme pain on the rock, in the snow, he feels hopeless. He remembers he is angry at his mum for leaving the family and sad that he split up with his girlfriend, Sarah. He recognises that Kenny, even though he's older and they have a special bond, has needs that are 'a lot to handle'.

With the river rising and no sign of Kenny, Nicky decides he must grit his teeth and somehow drag himself to safety. McGowan writes, 'I was moving slowly, so slowly, but I still jarred my leg a couple of times on juts of rock. It was like I'd been hit with an iron bar, and I bellowed out my pain and rage and frustration.'

As Nicky moves forward, he comes to a different part of the river and with a sinking heart he sees Kenny's hat floating in the river.

1.1.5 Reading, viewing and listening to texts

1 Circle the emotions you think Nicky is feeling at this moment.

Frustration	Ecstasy	Loneliness	Irritation	Boredom	Anger

As Nicky drifts in and out of consciousness, his thoughts become jumbled – thoughts about his mum and dad, Kenny, his dog Tina, and stories that he loved as a child. The final sentence of Chapter 17 ends with 'I lost all my hope.'

2 How you think the reader is feeling at this point in the story? What might they think is going to happen?

1.1.6 Expressing ideas and composing texts

Chapter 18 opens as Nicky wakes on a new day.

Complete one of the following activities.

Activity 1:

In the voice of Nicky, describe your hopes and fears about what this new day will bring.

OR

Activity 2:

In the voice of Kenny, describe your hopes and fears about what this new day will bring.

How can a single symbol enhance the narrative?

As you will have learnt previously, a symbol is an image, object or idea that holds significant meaning in a text. One important symbol in McGowan's novel is the **lark**.

You may know that the lark is particularly treasured for its beautiful song and for its skill of singing while in the air, not just when it is perched on a tree. Its song often symbolises **optimism** and **hope**.

1.1.7 Understanding and responding to texts A

Just when Nicky needs some hope and optimism, the lark arrives in the story – right on cue!

> And then I heard the sound. The mad, ecstatic music of the lark. I peered into the brightness and saw the small bird straining upwards, its flight not like the easy, carefree swooping of swallows and swifts. The lark's flight was all effort, as if hauling itself up by sheer will – a wanting, a yearning. To fly and to sing was work, it was grit. And it was beautiful. And then the lark flew so high it escaped the earth's gravity, and suddenly flying was no effort at all. And finally the lark was so high that I lost the song, and though I tried to keep my eye on the tiny dot in the blue forever, striving to keep my eyes open in case I couldn't find it again, at last I blinked, and my eyes opened not into the blue and gold but into the black.
>
> And then I understood that the lark wasn't a lark, but a soul, and that I was alone, and that a beautiful thing had just left this world.

1 What words/phrases do you think are particularly effective to characterise the lark and its music?

2 How do you interpret McGowan's meaning in the final sentence? How does Nicky's realisation make you feel?

3 In what way might the lark's effort be a metaphor for Nicky's own journey in the story? Justify your thinking with close reference to the passage.

1.1.8 Chapter reflection

1 Thinking back on this chapter, what are the top three things you have learnt about writing well that you will take forward?

2 Imagine you have been tasked with writing a 50-word review of this novel. What would you say?

3 Let's return to the central inquiry question: ***How does the novel explore the human condition?*** This chapter has encouraged you to understand that writers can use setting to convey the thoughts and feelings of characters. What emotions did you find most powerful in the novel?

4 Which part/s of the novel did you find revealed the true nature of the characters, Nicky and Kenny, most effectively for you? Explain your thinking in connection with the essential question.

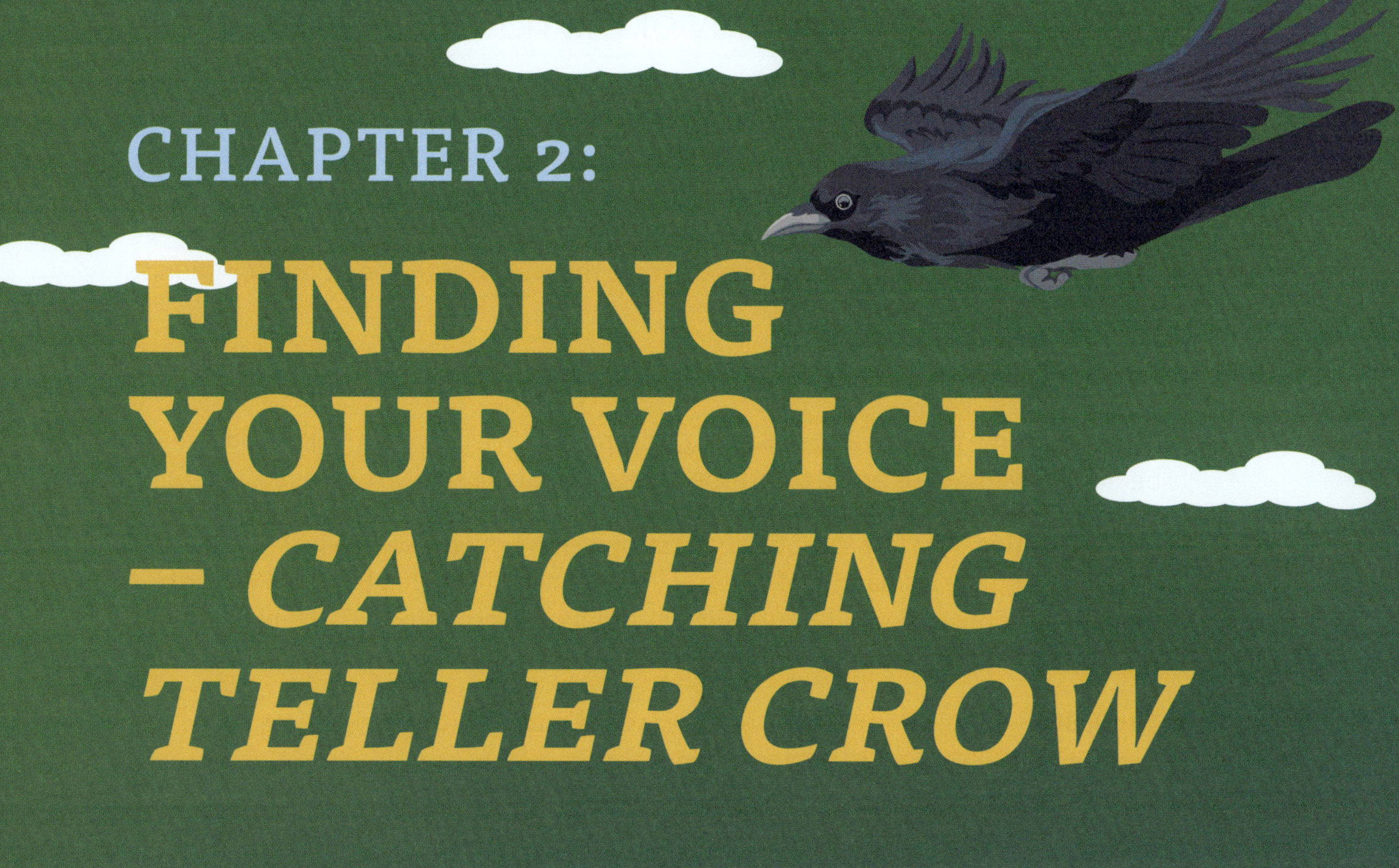

CHAPTER 2: FINDING YOUR VOICE – *CATCHING TELLER CROW*

Chapter overview

In this chapter, you will consider how the alternating narratives of the central characters Beth Teller and Isobel Catching underpin the novel *Catching Teller Crow*.

Success criteria: In this chapter, I will be successful when I can ...

- engage with diverse and complex perspectives and experiences, including those of Aboriginal and Torres Strait Islander peoples
- analyse how Aboriginal and Torres Strait Islander authors use figurative language and devices to represent culture, identity and experience
- examine how elements of focalisation and narrative voice can shape perceptions of meaning and apply this in my own texts, using an adventurous figurative vocabulary and varied sentences.

Chapter inquiry questions

- How can narrative voice influence the reader's perspective and engagement with the story?
- How can perspectives and experiences convey values and attitudes in a narrative?
- How can connotation, imagery and symbols represent culture and identity?

Key vocabulary

- Focalisation
- Narrative voice
- Alternating narrative
- Symbol

What's it all about?

This novel, by siblings Ambelin Kwaymullina and Ezekiel Kwaymullina, tells the story of a fire in a children's home and the subsequent discovery of a corpse. Michael Teller is brought in to investigate and discovers more than arson at the heart of a community. The setting is a small Australian town.

At the centre of the narrative are three voices:

Beth Teller – the ghost of a First Nations girl who died in a car crash. She accompanies her father everywhere, afraid that if she leaves, he will not survive her loss.

Isobel Catching – the last in a long line of strong First Nations women who is both the victim and the dismantler of a web of violence and abuse that has been woven by those in positions of power to catch First Nations girls and women. Catching is imbued with the power to move between the worlds of the living and the dead.

Sarah Blue – this final narrative is revealed to the reader through the voices of Catching and Teller. Sarah is represented in the story by a Crow.

These three voices weave a tale about how First Nations women have suffered because of colonial values, but it also offers hope for reconciliation and lasting change.

Scan the QR code. If you do not have the novel, you can listen to it here.

1.2.1 Warm-up

Let's experiment with focalisation, the perspective of writing.

Replay a conversation you have had with a friend or parent/guardian – this can be real or imagined. It might have been when you wanted to do something, to go out somewhere or with someone, and your friend or parent/guardian wanted you to do something else, or not go at all.

Reflect on this moment, then write your version – or justification – of events below.

How can narrative voice influence the reader's perspective and engagement with the story?

This question encourages you to think about how **narrative voice** and **focalisation** shape your emotional connection to the characters and your immersion in the plot.

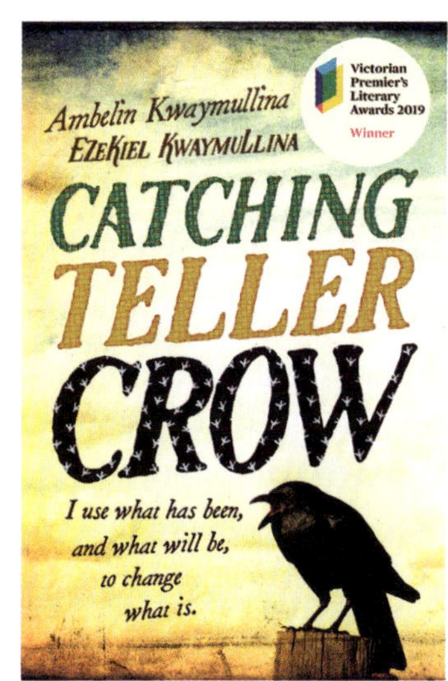

Focalisation refers to the *perspective* from which the story is told, while narrative voice refers to how the story is told.

These stylistic conventions also prompt you to think about the role of the reader in interpreting the story.

In *Catching Teller Crow*, the stories of Beth Teller, Isobel Catching and Sarah Blue are told and intertwined using an **alternating narrative**.

A dual narrative, also known as a multiple or alternating narrative, can be particularly effective in a novel to represent different perspectives and arguments. In this novel, it is also used to communicate a sense of authority.

In their simplest form, multiple narratives tell the story of the same event at the same time from different perspectives, using different voices. This is most effective when those voices are in opposition to one another or when one voice 'fills in the gaps' of the other, thus requiring the reader to need both voices to form a complete understanding of events.

1.2.2 Understanding and responding to texts B

The novel begins with Beth Teller's voice. It is through her that the reader meets her father, Michael Teller.

Read the passages from Chapter 1 of the novel and complete the activities.

He pressed his hand to his chest, out of breath from climbing up this rocky hill. There were a bunch of rock formations like this one around here, rising up from a flat red plain that was dotted with trees. I liked the trees. They were old and white and twisty, spiralling upward to fling out their leaves as if they were hoping to touch the sky. I liked the sky too; there seemed to be more of it here than in the city. There were no buildings to block it out. No big ones, anyway. We could see much of the town from where we stood: a sprawl of houses surrounded by the scattered trees, with a long river to the north. The town was covered in the same dust that coated everything, including our car and my dad's rumpled shirt and trousers. The dust hadn't touched my clothes, of course. My dress would always be as yellow and crisp as it had been on the day Auntie Viv drove me to the birthday party.

DISCUSS

Think about how the author has created a strong sense of place. Highlight the key words and phrases that stand out to you.

Dad took a step closer to the edge of the hill, gazing outwards.

'I don't think you're going to solve the case from up here,' I told him.

His gaze shifted in my direction. His eyes were bright with tears. Sometimes he couldn't even look at me without sobbing. Today the tears didn't fall. But I could hear them in his voice when he said, 'I miss you, Beth.'

'I'm right here, Dad.'

Except we both knew I wasn't. At least, not in the way he wanted me to be.

The accident had happened so fast. One minute I'd been sitting in Auntie Viv's sedan, everything normal. Then I'd heard the four-wheel drive ploughing through the bushes as it tore down the embankment. I'd looked up to see it hurtling at me, and ... nothing. I didn't remember the actual dying part. In fact, I *felt* as if I was still a living, breathing girl.

1 **A good opening to a story often introduces character/s to pique the reader's curiosity about them – perhaps their intriguing qualities, dilemmas or conflicts. This is known as 'the hook'.**

After reading this extract, what about these characters makes you interested?

____

____

____

____

2 **To engage the reader, a novel's opening often has a clear mood or atmosphere.**

Circle the word/s that best describe the mood in this extract.

sinister joyful mysterious brooding light-hearted conflicted

Beth Teller's voice is written in the first person and in the past tense. The advantage of the first-person narration is that it invites the reader to travel with Teller through her story and engage with her thoughts and feelings in an intimate way. However, the disadvantage is that the reader only sees events, characters and places through her eyes, which can be a limitation, especially if she doesn't have all the information or understand her experiences fully.

Catching Teller Crow is an unconventional detective story and the story gradually unfolds through the **alternating narrative**.

Isobel Catching is the second voice the reader hears in the story; her character is introduced in the third chapter, 'The Witness'. In the investigation, Michael Teller interviews Catching, believing her to be a witness to the fire in the children's home, but she piques the reader's interest with her words.

> **'But, when I start talking, you're gonna tell me there's no such thing as monsters and other-places ... This thing didn't even start with the fire ... It started with a sunset.'**

These words position the reader to hear Catching's version of events, but her voice is very different to Teller's. **Her narrative is written in the first person, in the present tense and in verse**. In her narrative, the author intertwines the past and present. The reader is encouraged to experience the present events with Catching, but also to understand how the past is significant in shaping her understanding of her history and culture as a young First Nations woman and how this impacts her identity.

This extract is from the start of Catching's narrative. She is on a road trip with her mother learning that she is part of a long line of strong women.

> **I'm not good with anger.**
> **It lights my blood like flames.**
> **I become fire.**
> **But on this road trip, Mum's taught me words that control**
> **fire.**
> **The names of the Catching women, from my great-great-**
> **grandma onwards.**
> ***Granny Trudy Catching ...***
> ***Nanna Sadie Catching ...***
> ***Grandma Leslie Catching ...***
> ***Mum ...***
> ***Me.***

3 As you read or listen to the novel, consider how the authors use these names to help Catching overcome her suffering. You can write down your ideas below.

____

____

____

____

____

____

1.2.3 Understanding and responding to texts A

After a road accident in which her mother is drowned, Catching is discovered, abducted by two men and imprisoned in a series of tunnels close to the children's home.

During her imprisonment, the suffering Catching endures is so great that her narrative is told through metaphor. This authorial choice gives authority to Catching's voice and creates empathy in the reader.

> They've got *wings*. Leathery. Grey.
> Their robes are grey too.
> Long robes, which hide their heads and bodies.
> Robes that blend with everything else and make their edges
> hard to see.
> Their faces are covered by white masks with human features.
> But they can't be human ...
>
> ... What are you?' I demand.
> They answer together, 'Fetchers.'
>
> ... 'I'm small and they're big.
> They have wings that fly.
> Claws that fetch.
> I have only me.

1 How do the authors use imagery to create a terrifying description of the 'Fetchers'?

2 Why do you think Catching believes the 'Fetchers' could not be human?

How can perspectives and experiences convey values and attitudes in a narrative?

Detective fiction has traditionally been established around particular conventions and many of these reinforce ideas of control and criminality that stem from Western European traditions of the nineteenth and twentieth centuries.

You can learn more about this by researching Van Dine's Rules for detective fiction.

Catching Teller Crow follows a tradition that dismantles many of the conventions of detective fiction. Van Dine stated that:

> **The problem of the crime must be solved by strictly naturalistic means. Such methods for learning the truth as slate-writing, ouija-boards, mind-reading, spiritualistic séances, crystal-gazing, and the like, are taboo.**
>
> **There must be but one detective – that is, but one protagonist of deduction – one deus ex machina.**

In many detective stories, from the 1920s onwards, the attitudes and values presented to the reader reflected a single, often male, detective who wielded intellectual power over the more inferior characters in the story until, through rational and scientific deduction, he solved the crime.

Ambelin and Ezekiel Kwaymullina have dismantled many of the genre's conventions by having more than one detective – both Michael and Beth Teller. In addition, Van Dine's absolutism of 'strictly naturalistic means' is challenged by the authors' creative use of ghosts and the supernatural, which also helps the reader to engage with Australia's colonial history.

1.2.4 Understanding and responding to texts A and C 

Michael Teller's words below show the values and attitude of the past.

> **'If a white girl had gone missing like that, just vanished on her way home from school –' he shook his head in disgust – 'there'd have been an outcry. It would have been on the news, in the papers, something everyone talked about on the street. Instead, the only people speaking for Sarah [aka Crow] – her family, her friend – were ignored.'**

1 **What is Teller's tone and how does the language used create it?**

Catching's perspective reminds the reader of both past and present attitudes towards social violence.

As you read the extracts below from the chapter 'The Two', think about the powerlessness of the captive girls and how that is conveyed.

> I'm being carried like a piece of meat ...
> Can't run. Can't fight. Only endure. Like always.

2 **How does the sentence structure here emphasise Catching's attitude to her situation?**

> His palm presses against my stomach.
> His fingers rip up my flesh.
> He digs for my soul ...
>
> No sound comes out of my mouth.
> It's all locked inside.

3 **How do the authors convey the lack of power that Catching has here against her abusers?**

How can connotation, imagery and symbols represent culture and identity?

Metaphor, simile and personification are used abundantly in *Catching Teller Crow*. As you read the novel, highlight these to remind you how rich language can be.

1.2.5 Understanding and responding to texts A

Let's revise!

Quotation	Metaphor, simile or personification?	How does this connect to culture and/or identity? Clue: you will write a better comment if you find the quotation in context. ☺
'Small towns can be like lakes: quiet and still on the surface, but with lots going on beneath.' (p. 69)		
'Her lips twisted into a snarl that said *back off* as clearly as if she'd shouted it.' (p. 54)		
'It lights my blood like flames. / I become fire.' (p. 27)		
'Aunty Jane had always called me her butterfly girl.' (p. 64)		
'I'm a glass thrown against rock. / Shattered. Bits of me everywhere. / I'll never find them all. / No one will.' (p. 108)		

Throughout the novel, the Kwaymullina duo uses symbols and motifs to convey suffering and destruction but also love, hope and family.

The following table lists some of the symbols used in the novel. See if you can find some examples from the text. Make sure you explain the connection between the symbol, your example and how it reflects ideas in the novel – particularly of identity and/or culture.

The first one has been done for you as an example. Fill the blank boxes with your own.

Symbol	Example	Connections
The children's home	'What had once been the children's home was now a pile of blackened timber' (p. 12)	The children's home is a symbol of a culture of abuse and violence against First Nations children spanning generations. At the start of the novel the home has been destroyed through fire – which can be seen as a force for both destruction and cleansing. Thus, this symbol foreshadows both the despair and the hope communicated by the narrators.
Birds/flying		
Fire		

1.2.6 Expressing ideas and composing texts A

It's your turn to put some of the ideas you have been learning about into practice by using symbols alongside an engaging narrative voice in your own writing.

Your goal: To write creatively with a clear sense of purpose and intention by:

- applying narrative voice to depict complex ideas and enhance reader engagement
- experimenting with figurative language to convey emotion
- using a variety of sentence lengths, types and complexity for effect
- using tense accurately and purposefully.

Your task: Use one of the symbols listed in the table above, to craft a piece of original writing in your English notebook or on paper. Use this symbol as a central feature that shapes meaning in your narrative or poem.

1.2.7 Chapter reflection

Reflect on how an appreciation of texts can be enhanced through re-reading and close or critical study.

1 Let's return to our essential inquiry question for this unit: ***How does the novel explore the human condition?*** The human condition refers to the experiences that shape our identity – both the good and the bad. What did you find was the most formative experience for Teller in the novel and why?

2 What did you find was the most formative experience for Catching in the novel and why?

3 Teller's Grandpa Jim says: 'Life doesn't move through time. Time moves through life.' How can you see this idea represented in the novel?

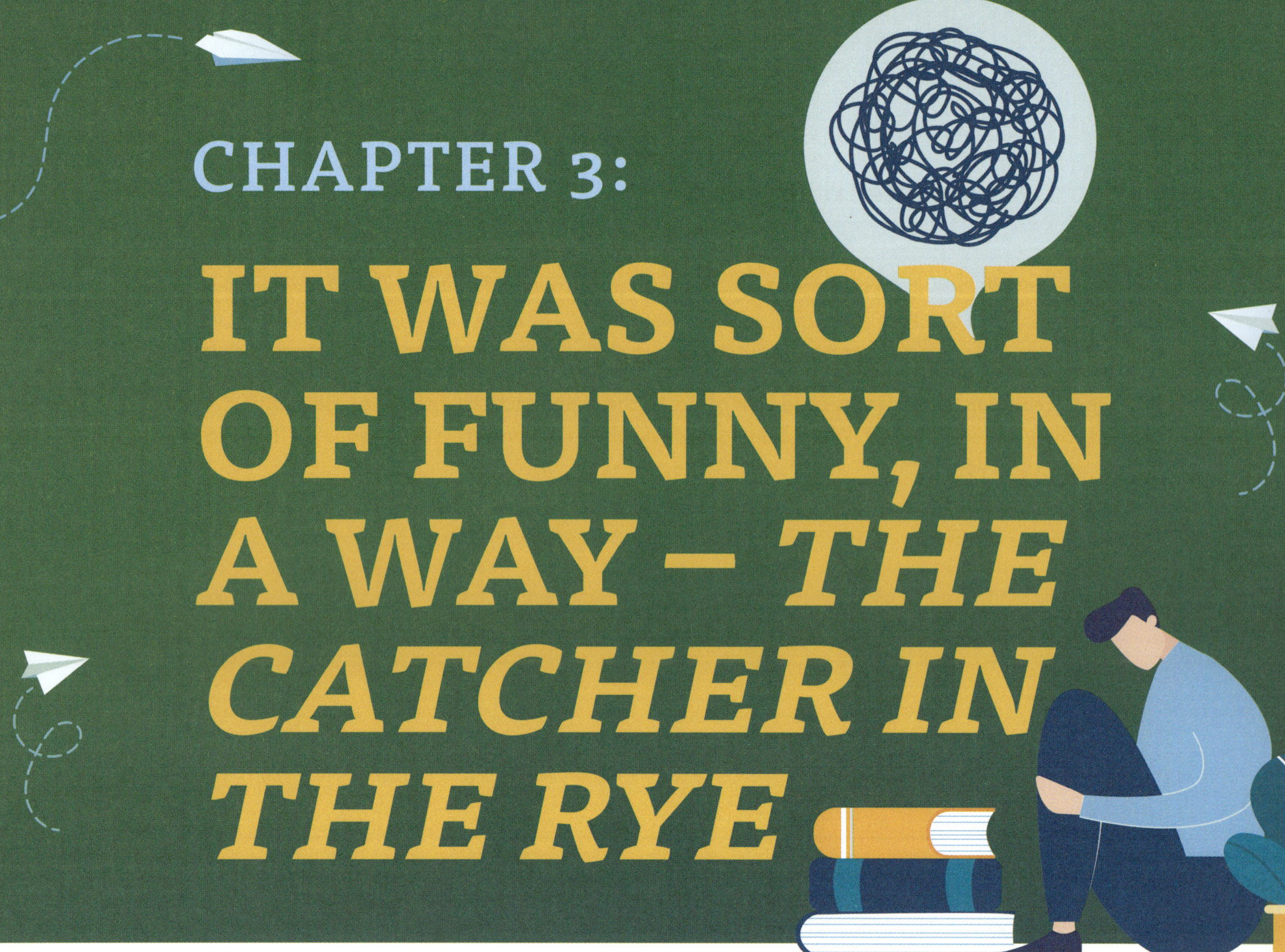

CHAPTER 3:

IT WAS SORT OF FUNNY, IN A WAY – *THE CATCHER IN THE RYE*

Chapter overview

In this chapter, you will learn about the Bildungsroman genre and how it is enjoyed by a wide range of audiences. You will study *The Catcher in the Rye* and examine how it is an example of this genre.

Success criteria: In this chapter, I will be successful when I can ...

- read to develop a deeper understanding of themes by revisiting and reinterpreting *The Catcher in the Rye*
- analyse how the use of language forms and features in *The Catcher in the Rye* has the capacity to create multiple meanings
- explore how characters in *The Catcher in the Rye* are lifelike constructions with whom audiences can connect and who can reflect, challenge or subvert values and attitudes
- analyse how elements of genre in *The Catcher in the Rye* can shape the way ideas and values are represented and perceived.

Chapter inquiry questions

- What is the Bildungsroman genre?
- How does the novel challenge or conform to the Bildungsroman genre?
- How does Salinger challenge and subvert the Bildungsroman protagonist/ character?

Key vocabulary

- Bildungsroman
- Characterisation
- Stream of consciousness

What is the Bildungsroman genre?

The Bildungsroman genre involves stories where the protagonist journeys from a troubled childhood to adult maturity. They are often stories that involve the progression from innocence to psychological and moral growth. The development of the character is the driving force of the plot and themes.

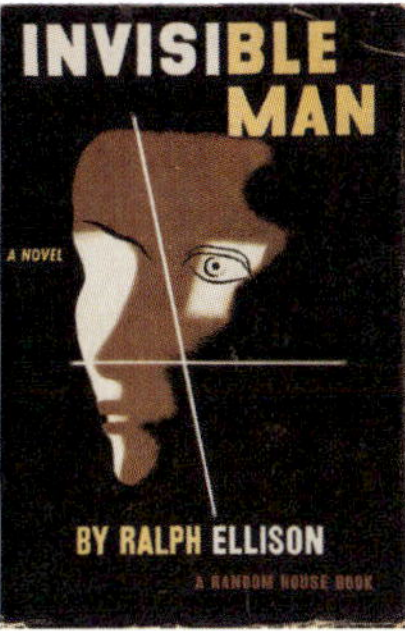

1.3.1 Warm-up

Discuss with a partner what the best book you've read is, and why.

The word **Bildungsroman** comes from German. *Bildung* means education and *Roman* means novel, so originally the word referred to 'a novel of education' or 'a novel of formation'.

J.D. Salinger's *The Catcher in the Rye* was published in 1951. It is a Bildungsroman story, narrated by seventeen-year-old Holden Caulfield, who has just been expelled from his school, Pencey Prep. With his unique voice and perspective, Holden recounts the days following his expulsion when he spends a few days in New York City before returning home. As we follow Holden on his journey, we see him attempt to grapple with loneliness, disaffection, grief and confusion, and try to come to terms with the realities and apparent 'phoniness' of the adult world.

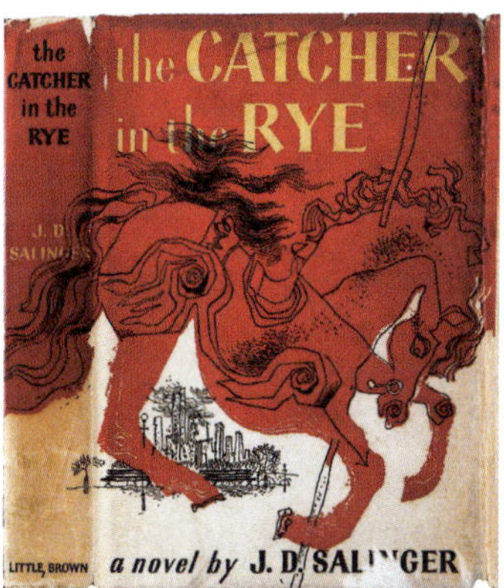

The Catcher in the Rye remains a classic piece of literature due to its powerful exploration of the complex journey of growing up.

Jerome David Salinger (1919–2010)

1.3.2 Reading, viewing and listening to texts

Based on the book's cover, its title and the synopsis, discuss these questions with a partner.

1 What do think the title means?

2 Reflect on your own experiences of being a teenager and growing up. What themes do you think Salinger might explore?

How does the novel challenge or conform to the Bildungsroman genre?

A Bildungsroman novel usually has a three-part structure: loss, journey and maturity. Bildungsroman stories begin with the protagonist in their youth, alone and alienated, and we often first meet them when they are experiencing a significant emotional loss.

1.3.3 Reading, viewing and listening to texts

Read the opening paragraph from Chapter 1 of *The Catcher in the Rye*.

IDENTIFY

Underline the evidence of this opening being typical of the Bildungsroman genre.

IDENTIFY

Through the subtle way that Salinger writes Holden's first-person narration, a lot of what is experienced is implied. Highlight the clues about what has happened and is happening to Holden.

If you really want to hear about it, the first thing you'll probably want to know is where I was born, and what my lousy childhood was like, and how my parents were occupied and all before they had me, and all that **David Copperfield** kind of crap, but **I don't feel like going into it**, if you want to know the truth. In the first place, that stuff bores me, and in the second place, my parents would have about two hemorrhages apiece if I told anything pretty personal about them. They're quite touchy about anything like that, especially my father. They're nice and all--I'm not saying that--but they're also touchy as hell. Besides, I'm not going to tell you my whole goddam autobiography or anything. I'll just tell you about this madman stuff that happened to me around last Christmas just before I got pretty run-down and had to come out here and take it easy. I mean that's all I told D.B. about, and he's my brother and all. He's in Hollywood. That isn't too far from this crumby place, and he comes over and visits me practically every week end. He's going to drive me home when I go home next month maybe. He just got a Jaguar. One of those little English jobs that can do around two hundred miles an hour. It cost him damn near four thousand bucks ...

PAUSE

Holden alludes to **David Copperfield**, by Charles Dickens, which is also a Bildungsroman novel narrated in the first person by David Copperfield, published in 1849. Explain the effect of Holden's allusion and the description 'kind of crap' that follows.

INTERPRET

Discuss Holden's phrase 'but I don't feel like going into it'. Why does he feel this way? What will he tell us?

1.3.4 Understanding and responding to texts

Read the rest of Chapter 1 and answer the following questions.

1 A Bildungsroman protagonist is sensitive and has a questioning nature, and doesn't fit in. Find evidence of this in Chapter 1.

2 The beginning of a Bildungsroman involves a tragedy or loss that significantly impacts the protagonist and initiates their journey. Is there a tragedy or loss? Identify and explain how it may contribute to Holden's early departure from school.

Holden

Bildungsroman stories typically represent protagonists who want to better themselves and leave behind childlike innocence. However, Salinger does not do this with his **characterisation** of Holden. Rather than trying to 'better' himself, Holden is sceptical about the adult world.

Holden's language provides the reader with ways into his experiences and psyche, allowing the reader to see things through his eyes. This is done through **stream of consciousness**. Holden narrates the events as he thinks of them. This helps Salinger to create a far more complex and authentic character.

> **VOCABULARY**
>
> **Characterisation**
> *noun:* the construction of a fictional character.
>
> **Stream of consciousness**
> *noun:* a literary style in which a character's thoughts and feelings are crafted as a continuous, uninterrupted flow.

1.3.5 Reading, viewing and listening to texts

Holden's voice: 'just about killed me'

Another way that we see things through Holden's perspective is through his unique voice, particularly his colloquial language and diction.

Writing worlds – a study of the novel

1 Discuss what you find interesting or unusual about Holden's style of speech.

2 Due to its context, unique style and narrative voice, the novel contains some unfamiliar words and phrases. Research some of these to learn their meanings.

Word	Meaning
Lousy	
Phony	
Chewed the rag	
Shot the bull	
Horsing around	
Chewing the fat	
Make it snappy	

In his first-person narration Holden uses language to mask and distance the intensity of his experiences and emotions. We must work harder to interpret what is happening and how Holden feels about it.

Let's look at some examples from Chapter 1.

IDENTIFY

Underline the hyperbolic language.

The reason **I was standing** way up on Thomsen Hill, instead of down at the game, was because I'd just got back from New York with the fencing team.

…

It was the last game of the year, and you were supposed to commit suicide or something if old Pencey didn't win. I remember around three o'clock that afternoon I was standing way the hell up on top of Thomsen Hill, right next to this crazy cannon that was in the Revolutionary War and all. You could see the whole field from there, and you could see the two teams bashing each other all over the place.

…

DISCUSS

Holden's grammar is unusual. Consider his tense choice, 'I was standing' instead of 'I stood'. Discuss the difference between these and how it makes Holden sound younger than he is.

Anyway, it was December and all, and it was cold as a witch's teat, especially on top of that stupid hill ... Anyway, I kept standing next to that crazy cannon, looking down at the game and freezing my ass off ...

...

It was icy as hell and I damn near fell down. I don't even know what I was running for--I guess I just felt like it. After I got across the road, I felt like I was **sort of** disappearing. It was that kind of a crazy afternoon, terrifically cold, and no sun out or anything, and you felt like you were disappearing every time you crossed a road.

...

I shook my head. I shake my head quite a lot. 'Boy!' I said. I also say 'Boy!' quite a lot. Partly because I have a lousy vocabulary and partly because I act quite young for my age sometimes. I was sixteen then, and I'm seventeen now, and sometimes I act like I'm about thirteen. It's really ironical, because I'm six foot two and a half and I have gray hair.

...

Grand. There's a word I really hate. It's a phony. I could puke every time I hear it.

...

Well, you could see he really felt pretty lousy about flunking me. So I shot the bull for a while.

...

The funny thing is, though, I was sort of thinking of something else while I shot the bull. I live in New York, and I was thinking about the lagoon in Central Park, down near Central Park South. I was wondering if it would be frozen over when I got home, and if it was, where did the ducks go. I was wondering where the ducks went when the lagoon got all icy and frozen over. I wondered if some guy came in a truck and took them away to a zoo or something. Or if they just flew away.

I'm lucky, though. I mean I could shoot the old bull to old Spencer and think about those ducks at the same time. It's funny. You don't have to think too hard when you talk to a teacher. All of a sudden, though, he interrupted me while I was shooting the bull. He was always interrupting you.

...

One of the biggest reasons I left Elkton Hills was because **I was surrounded** by phonies.

...

I didn't exactly flunk out or anything. I just quit, sort of.

DISCUSS

The phrase 'sort of' appears 179 times in the novel. Discuss how 'sort of' helps to create Holden's voice and suggests something about his psychological state.

IDENTIFY

Identify where you see examples of Holden's stream of consciousness.

INTERPRET

Holden often uses the passive voice: for example, 'I was surrounded'. Usually, we would use the active voice: 'Phonies surrounded me'. In active voice, the subject is actively involved in the action, but the passive voice creates distance between the subject and the action. Interpret what we learn about how Holden is feeling through the passive voice.

IDENTIFY

Holden also uses colloquial language to create an impression and to minimise and protect himself from his experiences. Highlight the colloquialisms. Think about how this language also shows Holden's unwillingness to grow up.

DISCUSS

Discuss your impression of Holden and how it is shaped by his language.

IDENTIFY

Can you find any other examples of where Holden creates distance through his language?

1.3.6 Expressing ideas and composing texts A

Write in Holden's voice by composing an extra scene for the novel.

How does Salinger challenge and subvert the Bildungsroman protagonist/character?

Journey

At some point in the early stages of a Bildungsroman novel, the protagonist is inspired to set out on a journey. This journey brings with it many challenges and conflicts, making the protagonist's path to maturity a difficult one. Typically, the protagonist is at odds with society, and they make many mistakes. However, these experiences shape the character of the protagonist as they slowly grow and mature.

1.3.7 Understanding and responding to texts

Typically, the classic departure moment in a Bildungsroman story involves the packing of bags, a serious moment of reflection and lots of crying.

1 Read Holden's departure.

Chapter 7

When I was all set to go, when I had my bags and all, I stood for a while next to the stairs and took a last look down the goddam corridor. I was **sort of** crying. I don't know why. I put my red hunting hat on, and turned the peak around to the back, the way I liked it, and then I yelled at the top of my goddam voice, 'Sleep tight, ya morons!' I'll bet I woke up every bastard on the whole floor. Then I got the hell out.

2 Holden's departure is a parody. Explain how Salinger subverts the typical departure moment and why.

____

____

____

____

1.3.8 Understanding and responding to texts A

Holden's figurative language and symbolism are 'ways in' to better understand and empathise with him and his journey. In groups, complete one of the following activities.

Allie's baseball mitt

Excerpt 1 [Chapter 5]

DISCUSS

Take note of the last sentence of excerpt 1. Discuss the effect of this.

My brother Allie had this left-handed fielder's mitt. He was left-handed. The thing that was descriptive about it, though, was that he had poems written all over the fingers and the pocket and everywhere. In green ink. He wrote them on it so that he'd have something to read when he was in the field and nobody was up at bat. He's dead now.

IDENTIFY

Holden's syntax reflects his spoken cadence, written as an **interior monologue**. The pace, pausing and emphasis vary. Identify the different types of sentences.

Excerpt 2 [Chapter 5]

IDENTIFY

Underline where you see the impact that Allie's death has had on Holden.

I was only thirteen, and they were going to have me psychoanalyzed and all, because I broke all the windows in the garage. I don't blame them. I really don't. I slept in the garage the night he died, and I broke all the goddam windows with my fist, just for the hell of it ... It was a very stupid thing to do, I'll admit, but I hardly didn't even know I was doing it, and you didn't know Allie.

DISCUSS

Discuss how we can interpret Holden and his relationship with his brother.

1 In excerpt 1, there is a striking shift in the last sentence. What do you notice about its tense? Explain what the present tense suggests to us about the nature of Holden's grief.

____

____

____

2 How does Salinger create empathy for Holden in these moments? Include quotations to support your response.

____

____

____

The red hunting hat

Excerpt 1 [Chapter 3]

DISCUSS

Discuss why Holden wears his hat with the peak over his eyes.

What I did was, I pulled the old peak of my hunting hat around to the front, then pulled it way down over my eyes. That way, I couldn't see a goddam thing.

IDENTIFY

Holden's syntax reflects his spoken cadence. The pace, pausing and emphasis vary. Identify the different types of sentences.

Excerpt 2 [Chapter 3]

... I took it off and looked at it. I sort of closed one eye, like I was taking aim at it. 'This is a people shooting hat,' I said. 'I shoot people in this hat.'

IDENTIFY

Underline where you see the impact that Allie's death has had on Holden.

DISCUSS

Discuss how we can interpret Holden and his relationship with his brother.

Excerpt 3 [Chapter 9]

I'd put on my red hunting cap when I was in the cab, just for the hell of it, but I took it off before I checked in.

1 Explain how the red hunting hat is used as a symbol to reflect how Holden is at odds with society.

2 Just like Allie's baseball mitt, the red hunting hat is a significant symbol that informs the reader of something about Holden that he is not able to explicitly communicate. Re-read the passages that refer to the hat and think about the different ways he wears his hat and what that may suggest. Analyse the hat's significance and what Salinger is highlighting about Holden.

Extension activity

Explore other symbols in the book, like the ducks, Jane and the kings, and suitcases. Outline what these symbols reveal to the reader about Holden.

How does the novel explore the theme of growing up (through the eyes of its protagonist)?

The Bildungsroman genre makes a great vehicle for authors to address timeless themes. This is what makes Bildungsroman stories so powerful. They capture something that we all experience – growing up.

Maturity

By the end of a Bildungsroman novel, we expect to see the protagonist displaying psychological development, change and maturity, having learnt from their mistakes and experiences.

1.3.9 Understanding and responding to texts A

Listen!

A big part of Holden's experience is that he feels like he is never heard or really understood. Throughout the novel the word 'listen' is frequently used by many characters, not just Holden.

1 **Find examples of when Holden says 'listen' but is not listened to. What could this be communicating about Holden's experience and the desire to be heard?**

____

____

____

____

2 **In Chapter 25, read the section where Holden and Phoebe go out together and Phoebe rides on the carousel. Identify the moment when Holden finally is listened to and explain the significance of his relationship with Phoebe.**

____

____

____

____

Comin thro' the rye

Holden's fantasy of being a 'catcher in the rye' also communicates the theme of growing up.

3 **Explain what Salinger is communicating through *The Catcher in the Rye*.**

____

____

____

____

4 **How does this theme reflect what many teenagers feel as they stand on the cusp of adulthood?**

____

____

____

____

5 **How is this theme expressed at the end of Chapter 25 when Holden watches Phoebe go around on the carousel?**

____

____

____

____

Usually at the end of a Bildungsroman novel, the protagonist finds an inner acceptance of themselves or a sense of belonging with the world. In *The Catcher in the Rye*, we learn that all the experiences on Holden's journey led him to a mental institution.

1.3.10 Reading, viewing and listening to texts

The book's ending has created a lot of debate and discussion, particularly about whether Holden has changed and developed as a character.

1 Read the last paragraph.

IDENTIFY

Underline the evidence of this closing being typical of the Bildungsroman genre.

D.B. isn't as bad as the rest of them, but he keeps asking me a lot of questions, too. He drove over last Saturday with this English babe that's in this new picture he's writing. She was pretty affected, but very good-looking. Anyway, one time when she went to the ladies' room way the hell down in the other wing D.B. asked me what I thought about all this stuff I just finished telling **you** about. I didn't know what the hell to say. If you want to know the truth, I don't know what I think about it. I'm sorry I told so many people about it. About all I know is, I sort of miss everybody I told about. Even old Stradlater and Ackley, for instance. I think I even miss that goddam Maurice. It's funny. Don't ever tell anybody anything. If you do, you start missing everybody.

INTERPRET

Who is the 'you' Holden refers to?

INTERPRET

Discuss the meaning of the last two sentences.

2 Consider the ambiguity of the last two sentences. Why do you think Salinger left them open to interpretation?

____

____

____

3 Does the ending reflect a typical Bildungsroman ending? Is it hopeful or sad? Does Holden learn anything?

____

____

____

1.3.11 Chapter reflection

1 How has your appreciation for *The Catcher in the Rye* been enhanced through re-reading and critical study?

2 'J. D. Salinger's *The Catcher in the Rye* captures what it is like to be a teenager.' To what extent do you agree?

3 The Bildungsroman has remained a popular genre. Why do you think it is still popular? Outline reasons for its universal appeal and reflect on how reading *The Catcher in the Rye* has increased your enjoyment of the genre.

4 Let's return to our central inquiry question for this unit: ***How does the novel explore the human condition?*** The human condition refers to the experiences that shape our identity. In your opinion, what did the novel highlight about the human condition?

Unit 1: **Summative assessment**

The summative assessment options below provide opportunities to demonstrate your achievement of the following outcomes and focus areas.

Outcome and focus area	EN5-RVL-01 Reading, viewing and listening to texts	EN5-URA-01 Understanding and responding to texts A	EN5-URB-01 Understanding and responding to texts B	EN5-URC-01 Understanding and responding to texts C	EN5-ECA-01 Expressing ideas and composing texts A	EN5-ECB-01 Expressing ideas and composing texts B
Content point	Reading, viewing and listening skills	Connotation, imagery and symbol	Theme	Genre	Writing	Planning, monitoring and revising
		Point of view		Literary value	Sentence-level grammar and punctuation	
		Characterisation				
		Narrative				
	Reading, viewing and listening for meaning					Reflecting
	Reading for challenge, interest and enjoyment		Argument and authority			
	Reflecting		Style			

Option 1: *Lark*

PART 1

As you worked through your study of *Lark* you were asked to create two story openings. Your task now is to choose one of these and develop it into a complete narrative with a clear orientation, complication, climax and resolution. Remember, too, that characters must be credible to engage your audience.

Be guided by the following questions to plan and write your creative piece.

- Which opening 'hook' will you use to engage your reader?
- How will you establish a clear and interesting narrative voice for your reader?
- How will you create believable and engaging characters through action and dialogue?
- How could you establish a realistic setting that is appropriate for the action taking place?
- Remember to write clearly, but think about how your vocabulary choices can also be adventurous. For example, have you used figurative phrases or a motif?

PART 2

Reflect on the choices you have made in your creative piece.

- What intentional linguistic choices, such as a motif, have you made to engage your audience in either the characters, setting or action of your piece?
- Have some of your choices been more successful than others? Why do you think this might have been?

Option 2: *Catching Teller Crow*

In the novel *Catching Teller Crow*, the voice the reader does not hear directly is that of Sarah Blue, the first victim of Alexander Sholt and Derek Bell. In the novel Sarah is known as Crow. In this task you are going to experiment with creating Crow's voice – in verse, in prose or through images.

PART 1

Re-write a section of the novel through Crow's eyes OR create a new piece, connected to the novel, which details her feelings and experiences.

To prepare, revisit the sections of the novel where she features in either the narrative of Beth Teller or the narrative of Isobel Catching to get a sense of her character.

Keep detailed notes while you do this.

Be guided by the following questions to plan and write your piece.

- Which particular stylistic features from the novel, such as repeated words, phrases or questions, can you use?
- How can you show both her vulnerability and her strength through your words and/ or images?
- Can you link her voice to her name, Crow, through imagery or a particular motif?

PART 2

Reflect on the choices you have made in your creative piece.

- What intentional linguistic choices have you made to create Crow's voice?
- Have some of your choices been more successful than others? Why do you think this might have been?
- How would hearing Crow's voice, as you have written it, have enriched the novel?

Option 3: *The Catcher in the Rye*

Demonstrate an understanding of the Bildungsroman genre and Holden Caulfield's character by crafting a narrative in which he visits your place of residence for three days.

PART 1

Write a Bildungsroman narrative in Holden's voice, chronicling his experiences during the three days. Capture Holden's distinct language, tone and perspective. Use Holden's favourite expressions and colloquialisms, as well as his use of stream of consciousness, tense and the passive voice.

Introduce at least one original character from your life for Holden to interact with during his stay. Develop dialogue and interactions that reflect Holden's views on authenticity and phoniness, and his general attitude towards people.

Be guided by the following questions to plan, write and produce your narrative.

- Which **character/s?** will you introduce into your story?
- Think about the location, surroundings and other specific details about your place of residence. What might Holden notice or comment on?
- Create a daily itinerary for Holden during his three-day visit. What activities would he engage in? Where would he go? Think about Holden's preferences and interests.
- What **narrative conventions** from the Bildungsroman genre will you include in your narrative?
- What stylistic features from *The Catcher in the Rye* can you experiment with in your narrative?

PART 2

Peer feedback

Share excerpts from your writing with a peer and seek feedback on how well you captured Holden's voice and whether your imagined scenarios align with the character as portrayed in the novel. Apply this feedback to refine your composition.

PART 3

Reflection

After completing your narrative, reflect on the experience and write a reflection about the decisions you made to capture Holden's voice. How did you find writing in Holden's voice? What stylistic features did you use and why? What challenges did you face, and what insights did you gain into his character?

Assessment as learning: self-assessment

Does my composition:

- ☐ use figurative language and devices to represent culture, identity and experience?
- ☐ create an engaging personal voice to represent a perspective and communicate a sense of authority?
- ☐ experiment with stylistic features that shape its purpose?

How effectively did my plan and drafts help me to draft and revise my composition?

____

____

What are two strengths of my response?

____

____

What area/s of my response do I need to refine further?

____

____

The power of film

Unit inquiry question:
How does film captivate audiences and provoke deeper thinking about themes and ideas?

Students will learn about film and how it is used to represent ideas, characters and themes. Students will examine the satirical film *Zoolander* and analyse how it presents a particular viewpoint.

Students will explore the nature of film adaptations through a study of Matthew Vaughn's film *Stardust*.

In the last chapter of this unit, students will have the opportunity to examine the enduring appeal of the fictional character Sherlock Holmes.

This unit has been broken into three chapters, which each look at a different aspect of texts and the world and raise additional inquiry questions.

CHAPTER 4

The depth of shallow – *Zoolander*

An examination of satire and stereotypes in the film *Zoolander*.

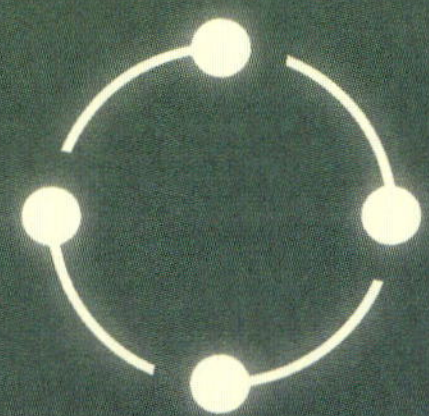

CHAPTER 5

From page to screen – *Stardust*

An investigation into the nature of film adaptations through an analysis of the film *Stardust*.

CHAPTER 6

Will the real Sherlock Holmes stand up?

An exploration of the evolution of Sherlock Holmes through film.

The learning activities within each chapter and the summative assessment options (on pages 81–83) provide opportunities to assess student achievement of the following outcomes.

Outcome and focus area	Content point
EN5-RVL-01 **Reading, viewing and listening to texts**	**Reading, viewing and listening for meaning**
	Draw on prior knowledge of texts to question, challenge and deepen understanding of both new and familiar texts
	Analyse the main ideas and thematic concerns represented in texts
	Reflecting
	Reflect on how reading, viewing and listening to texts has informed and inspired learning
EN5-URA-01 **Understanding and responding to texts A**	**Representation**
	Analyse how contextual, creative and unconscious influences shape the composition, understanding and interpretation of all representations
	Characterisation
	Explore how characters in texts can be lifelike constructions with whom audiences establish intellectual and emotional connections, and can be perceived to reflect, challenge or subvert particular values and attitudes
EN5-URB-01 **Understanding and responding to texts B**	**Theme**
	Appreciate the role of the audience in perceiving themes and how these themes can offer insights into an author's perspective
	Argument and authority
	Analyse how subjectivity and objectivity are constructed in texts to form arguments, and how these can represent particular perspectives
	Appreciate how authority over meaning in texts, such as multimodal and interactive texts, can be distributed, and is a negotiation between acts of authorship, publication and interpretation

EN5-ECA-01 **Expressing ideas and composing texts A**	**Speaking**
	Select effective rhetorical strategies to position an audience and evoke an emotional response
	Text features
	Use the structural conventions of persuasive texts to purposefully justify opinions and develop expanding arguments, including a focused opening and thesis, logically sequenced elaboration paragraphs, and a conclusion that synthesises complex ideas
EN5-ECB-01 **Expressing ideas and composing texts B**	**Planning, monitoring and revising**
	Develop an effective thesis for extended analytical and persuasive texts that is based on critical thinking about a text or topic
	Plan a progressive sequence of arguments or ideas, and set goals at conceptual, whole text and paragraph levels
	Reflecting
	Evaluate own ability to plan, monitor and revise during the composition process, and how this can improve clarity, cohesion and effect

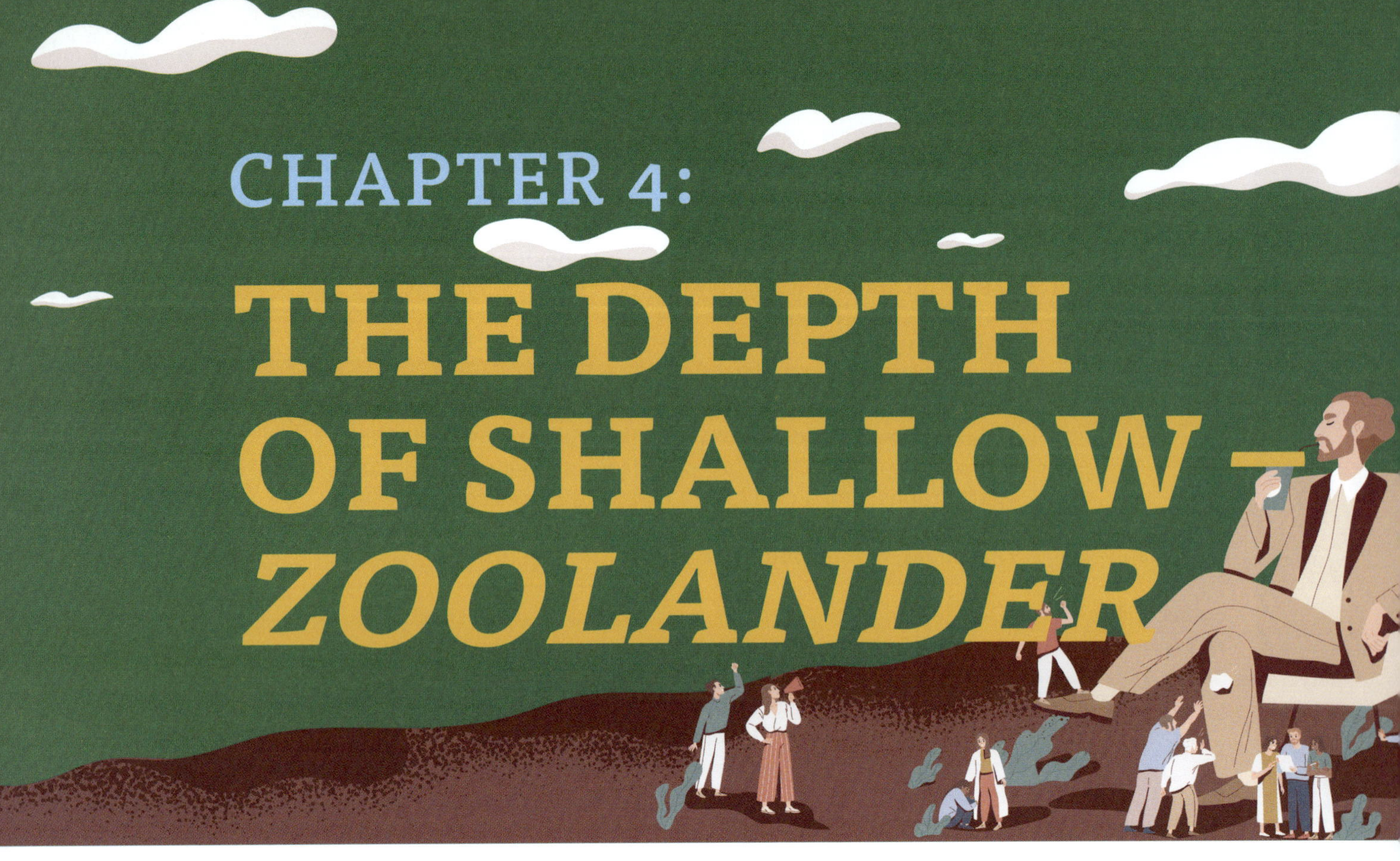

CHAPTER 4: THE DEPTH OF SHALLOW – *ZOOLANDER*

Chapter overview

In this chapter, you will examine the satirical film *Zoolander*, which humorously delves into the fashion industry's stereotypes. You will view, interpret and explain how film elements are used to convey a particular viewpoint. ***In order to successfully complete this chapter, you will need to watch the film as a class or individually.***

Success criteria: In this chapter, I will be successful when I can ...

- draw on prior knowledge of texts to question, challenge and deepen understanding of both new and familiar texts
- analyse the themes represented in film and how they offer insights into a director's perspective
- analyse how contextual, creative and unconscious influences shape the composition, understanding and interpretation of all representations in films
- explore how characters are constructions and can reflect, challenge or subvert particular values and attitudes
- reflect on how reading, viewing and listening to texts has informed and inspired learning.

Chapter inquiry questions

- How does context influence the creation and interpretation of representations in films?
- How do characters embody and challenge stereotypes?
- How does the film explore themes through its characters?
- How does the film use satire to present an argument?

Key vocabulary

- Representation
- Context
- Stereotypes

How does context influence the creation and interpretation of representations in films?

Before watching the film

'Did you ever think that maybe there's more to life than being really, really ... really ridiculously good looking?' (Derek Zoolander)

Zoolander (2001) is a satirical comedy directed by and starring Ben Stiller. Focussing on the fashion industry and stereotypes associated with it, its main character is world famous, dim-witted supermodel, Derek Zoolander (Ben Stiller). In the film, fashion industry big shot Jacobim Mugatu and Derek's agent Maury Ballstein are hired by some businesspeople who want to stop the Prime Minister of Malaysia from passing new laws that could hurt their businesses. Mugatu and Maury scheme to control Zoolander's mind and make him do something terrible to the prime minister.

2.4.1 Warm-up

What are your favourite types of film? Explain.

2.4.2 Reading, viewing and listening to texts

Film posters

1 Study the film posters.

2 Respond to the following questions to help you analyse and compare how ideas about the film are communicated.

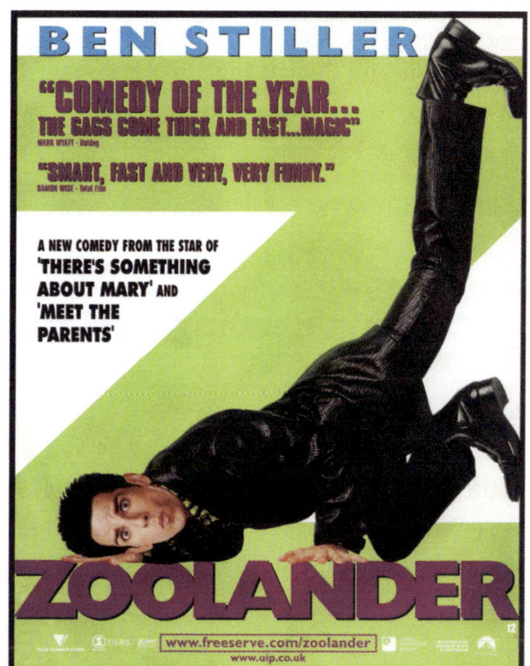

Ideas What do you see? What is happening?		
Visual features Note down what you notice about: camera angle, shot distance, gaze (offer/demand), colour, mood, salient feature and vectors.		
Layout What is in the background? Where is the subject placed in the shot?		

Film trailer

3 Using YouTube, watch the film trailer.

4 After studying the posters and watching the film trailer, you will have some ideas of what you think are the film's themes, tone and style. Write down your ideas.

5 What do you think is the film's message?

2.4.3 Reading, viewing and listening to texts

Think – Pair – Share

What is context?

1 Think about this question, then turn to a peer and discuss your answers.

Context and the text itself work together to create meaning. To really understand context, we need to go beyond just the words on the page and think about the world when the text was made and how people reacted to it. This means considering the following:

Composers – historical events, a composer's personal life, and their ways of seeing the world, all influence the creation of a text.

Responders – the ways a person sees the world in the moment they encounter a text influence how they respond to it.

Texts – texts influence and are influenced by other texts.

CONTEXT

Context is all the things that influence the composers of a text and audience at the time of their production and the time of their reception.

VOCABULARY

Context
noun: literally means 'what comes with the text' – and texts carry a lot of baggage.

Ben Stiller

The situations and backgrounds of the composer can change how we understand and feel about the same story or message. Let's take a look at Ben Stiller and his context to better understand how these factors have influenced the creation of and **representations** in the film.

Ben Stiller (born in New York City, 1965) is an American actor, comedian and filmmaker. His parents are both comedians and actors. Reflecting on his childhood, Stiller commented, 'In some ways, it was a show-business upbringing – a lot of traveling, a lot of late nights – not what you'd call traditional.' Early in his career, Stiller created **mockumentaries** and appeared on several comedy TV shows. He then began acting in films and even directing them.

VOCABULARY

Representation
noun: the description or depiction of someone or something.

Mockumentary
noun: a television show or film which takes the form of a serious documentary in order to satirise its subject.

2.4.4 Reading, viewing and listening to texts

1 **Based on your research, hypothesise how you think context influenced Stiller's decision to make *Zoolander*, as well as its form and ideas.**

Share your response.

What's really interesting is that when the film was first released, it was not well received. Critics hated it. The *Washington Post* described it as 'a one-joke movie', while *Time Out* wrote that it was 'a vanity comedy that fails at every level'. A significant event occurred just two weeks before *Zoolander* was released in America, which had a huge impact on how audiences responded to the film. This was the 9/11 terror attacks. 'It was such a hard time with comedy,' said Christine Taylor. 'Laughing might be a remedy in the moment, but the truth of the matter is, people weren't ready.' Ben Stiller agreed, adding, 'It was a weird time.'

Even though the film was a critical flop, it became a huge pop culture success. It gained a strong following among audiences for its humour and catchphrases.

2 **Look up some reviews of the film online. Find one negative and one positive review. Discuss with a partner some of the following:**

- What are the main points highlighted in each review?
- Are there any points on which both critics agree? Any aspects where their opinions significantly differ?
- How do you think the critics' personal preferences and biases might have influenced their reviews?

2.4.5 Understanding and responding to texts A

The opening scene

1 **Watch the opening scene, once without sound and then again with sound. Use the table to record your observations while viewing the opening.**

	What did you see? *Note down what you observed – camera movement, angles, shots, lighting, setting, characters, music, dialogue, etc.*	**What did you think?** *Note down what you thought or inferred based on your observations.*
First viewing – without sound		
Second viewing – with sound		

2 Make connections: What other films did the opening scene remind you of?

3 Considering the purpose of an opening scene, how effective do you think this opening is? Does it fit with the rest of the film?

How do characters embody and challenge stereotypes?

In his representation of male models, Stiller is relying on a common stereotype: attractive people must be 'empty-headed'. These characters are shown to be simple-minded, naïve and misguided. Stiller is also relying on another stereotype: those who are interested in fashion must be superficial. We see this through the way he represents the fashion designer, Mugatu.

2.4.6 Reading, viewing and listening to texts

During the 1980s, the term 'supermodel' became popular as models started to reach celebrity status. By the 1990s, the fashion industry was very popular and there was an obsession with the fashion world. Supermodels were a household name, and models started to appear on talk shows, in magazines and in films.

Research supermodels in the 1990s.

Christie Brinkley in studio publicity still from *National Lampoon's Vacation*

1 Who were the big names?

2 Are supermodels still popular today? Why or why not?

2.4.7 Understanding and responding to texts A

Derek

'... without Derek Zoolander, male modelling wouldn't be what it is.'

In the first ten minutes of *Zoolander* all the main characters are introduced: Derek, Mugatu, Hansel, Matilda, and Maury Ballstein. Ben Stiller and Drake Sather co-wrote the script and developed the character of Derek Zoolander. By taking the common stereotype of the 'dumb model' to the extreme, they created a humorous character.

Let's take a closer look at Derek.

1 Watch the opening scene where we meet Derek.

2 What do we learn about Derek when he says, 'It would have to be the first time I went through the second grade'?

---

3 Identify an example of satire in the opening scene and explain how it helps create Derek's character.

---

4 Identify an example of Derek saying something humorous in this scene. What does it reveal about his character?

---

5 Do you think Derek is a likeable character? Explain why/why not.

Touching your roots

Derek's character is exaggerated further when he decides to retire and return home to Southern New Jersey. Even Stiller's depiction of Southern New Jersey as a coal mining wasteland is humorous (and not accurate!).

6 Study this film still of the moment when Derek goes to the coal mine to find his father.

7 Describe Derek's clothing and the items he carries along the dirt road.

____

____

8 Explain how contrast is created between Derek and his surroundings. What is this shot seeking to suggest about Derek?

____

____

Derek is also presented as being 'unmanly', which challenges the concept of gender at the time. This is also highlighted in this scene when we meet Derek's father and brothers, and when Derek works in the mine.

9 Watch the montage of Derek working in the mine, once without sound and then again with sound. Use the following table to record your observations while viewing this scene.

	What did you see? *Note down what you observed – camera movement, angles, shots, lighting, setting, characters, music, dialogue, sounds, body language, etc.*	**What did you think?** *Note down what you thought or inferred based on your observations.*
First viewing – without sound		
Second viewing – with sound		

10 In what ways is Derek presented as being the opposite of his father?

11 List examples of how Derek is shown to not fit in with the hard physical labour of the mine and the 'blokey' culture of the bar.

12 What comment is the film making about masculinity?

Scan the QR code to access an interview activity with Hansel.

How does the film explore themes through its characters?

Through *Zoolander*, Stiller comments on and critiques aspects of popular culture and the fashion industry. Let's now look at how he uses satire and characters to communicate his perspective.

2.4.8 Understanding and responding to texts B

Beauty and superficiality

Examine a variety of scenes from *Zoolander* that highlight popular culture's obsession with appearance, such as Derek's reflection, Derek's interview, Mugatu's manipulation of Derek, and the Walk-Off. These scenes demonstrate Stiller's critique on society's obsession with beauty, the absurd and unrealistic beauty standards perpetuated by the fashion industry, and the valuing of superficial attributes over substance and character.

The characters' behaviour and costumes are cleverly created to reinforce these ideas, especially Derek, Hansel and Mugatu. They are exaggerated to the point where they appear ridiculous.

Watch each scene and record your notes in the following table. The first one has been done for you.

Scene	What happens in this scene?	What ideas about beauty and superficiality are revealed?	Where do you see this?	How does it communicate this theme? *Consider the construction of characters, camera framing and angles, music, dialogue and editing.*
Derek's reflection monologue	Derek gazes at his reflection in a puddle and questions the purpose of his existence.	This moment shows us the shallowness of Derek's identity as it is only defined by his appearance.	Derek asks, 'Who am I?'	To highlight Derek's superficiality, the scene depicts Derek being drawn to and gazing at his reflection. The camera frames Derek in a close-up shot for the audience to be closer to his emotional turmoil and confusion, but when his reflection responds with 'I don't know', the audience is reminded of Derek's inability to 'ponder' and think deeply on complex issues. The puddle splashing in his face straight after this moment undermines Derek's quest to be taken seriously.
Scene 2				
Scene 3				
Scene 4				

How does the film use satire to present an argument?

You learnt about satire in the Year 9 workbook, Unit 4 Chapter 3. To refresh, satire uses humour, irony and wit to **ridicule** the subject and to comment on or criticise society.

Let's examine some scenes from the film to learn how satire is used to critique aspects of fashion, consumerism and celebrity culture.

2.4.9 Understanding and responding to texts A

Ridiculous designer clothes

Before you plunge into examining the satire of the fashion show scene, you would benefit from having a bit of context. It's important to understand the target of Stiller's satire.

1 Oscar Wilde (Irish wit, poet and dramatist) once said, 'Fashion is a form of ugliness so intolerable that we have to alter it every six months.' Discuss with a friend what you think Wilde means here. Do you agree?

2 Use the internet to conduct some quick research on 'worst catwalk outfits' or 'ridiculous designer clothes'. Explain why you think designers create clothes that are expensive and aren't really designed to be worn by the average person. Do you think people would wear them? Why or why not?

Derelicte fashion show

3 At the beginning of the fashion show, Katinka grabs Matilda and says, 'Glad you could join us, Kmart. Lucky for you, there is no dress code.'

How is Katinka ridiculing Matilda's clothes through calling her 'Kmart'? What attitudes about fashion is Stiller highlighting here?

4 To introduce the show, Mugatu's voice recording is played: 'I am vile spew of the wretched masses. I am really, really dirty ... I am Derelicte!'

A model pops out of a cardboard box, which turns into the skirt of her outfit, and walks down the runway.
Consider the title for Mugatu's fashion collection, 'Derelicte', and Mugatu's introduction. What word is the title playing on and why is it spelt and pronounced differently?

5 What comment is Stiller making about the fashion industry through this title, the clothes and the models' presentations?

6 Analyse how the Derelicte fashion show satirises the fashion industry's treatment of social issues, specifically homelessness.

2.4.10 Chapter reflection

This chapter has encouraged you to understand how film can engage audiences to think and reconsider their views.

1 Do you think that a satirical film is an effective medium to make an audience think and challenge their assumptions?

2 How has studying *Zoolander* influenced your perception of the fashion industry and popular culture?

3 Let's return to the central inquiry question: ***How does film captivate audiences and provoke deeper thinking about themes and ideas?***

Outline the relevance of the film's themes in today's society. How might the satire presented in *Zoolander* still resonate with contemporary discussions on celebrity culture, industry manipulation and societal expectations? Discuss as a group.

CHAPTER 5:

FROM PAGE TO SCREEN – *STARDUST*

Chapter overview

In this chapter, you will explore the nature of film adaptations through a study of Matthew Vaughn's film *Stardust*. You will learn about the difference between adaptation, appropriation and transformation. You will think about what books you have read and films you have viewed to question, challenge and deepen your understanding of why books are adapted into films. ***In order to successfully complete this chapter, you will need to watch the film as a class or individually.***

Success criteria: In this chapter, I will be successful when I can ...

- draw on prior knowledge of texts to question, challenge and deepen understanding of both new and familiar texts
- analyse the themes represented in film and how they offer insights into a director's perspective
- analyse how contextual, creative and unconscious influences shape the composition, understanding and interpretation of all representations in films
- explore how characters are constructions that can reflect, challenge or subvert particular values and attitudes
- appreciate how authority over the meaning of a text is malleable
- reflect on how reading, viewing and listening to texts has informed and inspired learning.

Chapter inquiry questions

- Why are books adapted?
- Can a film adaptation ever be better than the book?
- How well have the themes been rendered in the film?

Key vocabulary

- Adaptation
- Fidelity
- Non-diegetic

Why are books adapted?

When we consider the world of film adaptations, it's important to be aware of the factors that influence how and why books are adapted into films.

These are:

- **Audience:** An audience comes with different expectations and receives a text through various perspectives. These viewpoints significantly shape the composer's decisions regarding the text, language, structure and form, ultimately impacting the main messages they want to share.
- **Context:** We can't avoid context. It's crucial to acknowledge that the surroundings of a text significantly impact its creation and our understanding of and reactions to it.
- **Purpose:** One of the biggest factors is the **reason** the text was created. Texts can serve multiple purposes, and understanding these intentions can significantly enhance your interpretation of the content.

2.5.1 Warm-up

There was once a young man who wished to gain his Heart's Desire.
And while that is, as beginnings go, not entirely novel (for every tale about every young man there ever was or will be could start in a similar manner) there was much about this young man and what happened to him that was unusual, although even he never knew the whole of it.
The tale started, as many tales have started, in Wall.

Stardust, Neil Gaiman

Continue the story.

Often, the choice to adapt a book into a film will demonstrate that some books are 'valued' more than others. We will explore the film adaptation of *Stardust* and consider why books are adapted, how context influences the creation and interpretation of representations in films, what ideas have been carried forward into the film despite the change in context, and what responsibilities the film director has to the original text.

But, before we start, take a moment to reflect on your own attitudes towards books and film adaptations.

2.5.2 Reading, viewing and listening to texts

Complete this survey.

	True	False
I get excited when one of my favourite books is adapted into a film.		
I shy away from seeing films adapted from books I really love.		
I always watch the film before reading the book.		
I don't read books. I prefer to watch the film adaptation.		
Film adaptations ruin the book.		
A film adaptation is always better than the book.		
There are some film adaptations that should never have been done.		
You just have to separate the movie from the book and think of it as something different.		
Hollywood adapts books to films because it's easier than coming up with original stories.		

1 Compare your answers with those of a partner. Were they the same? Which responses were different and why?

2 In an interview, Neil Gaiman (author) said, '... books and films are so different. Films occur in real time, they are one experience, they take two hours to happen and they play out and you see things and learn things. With a book, you have this peculiar experience in the back of somebody's head. You know, you've written something, but you only used words and now they are making their own film in their head, and if its good, it's better than anything you could ever make ... but for me books are kind of perfect because they involve no compromises at all.'

3 To what extent do you agree with Gaiman? Write a persuasive paragraph arguing for your perspective in response to Gaiman.

What is an adaptation?

Before we plunge into exploring the benefits and limitations of film adaptations, it's important to understand the difference between an adaptation, an appropriation and a transformation. You might have heard these terms before, and some people often use them synonymously. However, each one has a slightly different meaning.

2.5.3 Reading, viewing and listening to texts

Complete the following table. For each term, explain **what** it means, outline examples of **when** it is used, and explain **why** it is used (this is where you consider the purpose).

Term	What	When	Why
Adaptation	To transfer (adapt) a written work into a feature film. The only changes to the original that are made are for the purposes of the new form.	Novels are frequently adapted for films. For example,	To bring a text to a broader audience. Some audiences will be more likely to watch a film rather than read a book (unfortunately!).
Appropriation		Borrowing from a novel to create a film; updating the material to suit a modern audience. For example,	Some stories are just *too good* to let disappear.

Term	What	When	Why
Transformation	To change ('transform') the original material to suit a different purpose and fit a new context. To make a new text that is not reliant on the original for it to be appreciated or understood.	For example,	

Why are books adapted?

Adaptations are often created to attempt to appeal to an already existing commercial audience (for example, the *Harry Potter* books already had an audience). This is a sure way to make a lot of money. Sometimes, a filmmaker has attached some personal meaning to a book or play and it's been their dream to see it made as a film. Other times, adaptations try to capitalise on the innovation and novelty of a less well-known author, or seek the 'prestige' of adapting some literary classic. Interestingly, film adaptations of books earn more at the box office compared with films with original screenplays.

Whenever adaptations become part of the conversation, invariably the question of 'faithfulness' raises its head, and the more literary or popular the book, the more emphatic are the questions of **fidelity**. Can adaptations be appreciated on their own?

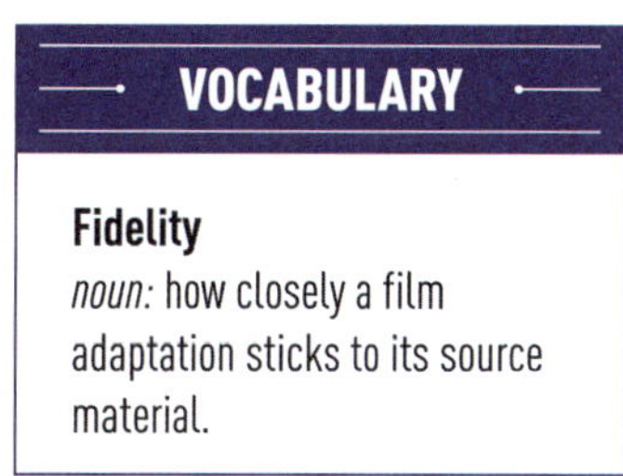

Some stories are just too good to do once

Adaptations often bear a negative perception: they're seen as recycled, repeated stories, or even stolen, lacking originality, and merely crafted from existing material. But is that always the case? One of the reasons books are adapted is that some stories are just great stories, and they will continue to resonate with us throughout time. Moreover, adaptations can reveal the original in a new way. Sometimes, we want to go back to the original and compare it with the adaptation – to see what's changed and why.

2.5.4 Reading, viewing and listening to texts

The film adaptation of Neil Gaiman's novel *Stardust* is a great example of this.

	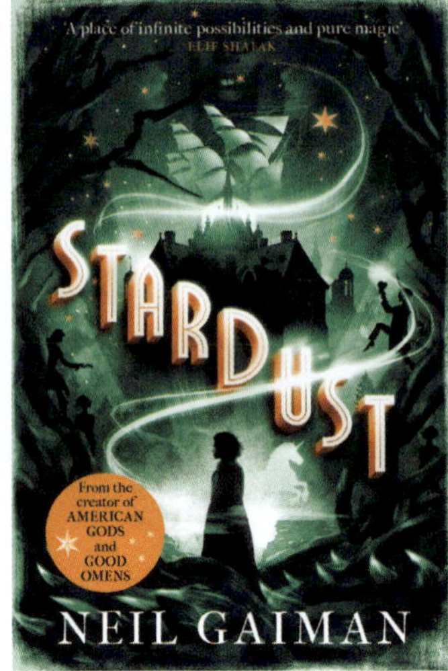	
1997	**1999**	**2007**
Stardust was first published by DC as an illustrated novel. It was written by Neil Gaiman and illustrated by Charles Vess.	*Stardust* was republished as a conventional novel without the illustrations.	After a few disappointing attempts, *Stardust* was adapted into a film by Matthew Vaughn.

The story of Stardust has gone through many transformations. Not only was it originally published as an illustrated novel and a traditional novel, it has also been made into a radio drama and a film. This demonstrates that there's an enduring appeal to this story – whether it's the romance, the characters or the adventurous narrative – that continues to captivate audiences without losing its allure.

1 Look at the book covers and film poster for *Stardust*. For each one, outline what you think is being communicated about the plot, genre, characters and themes.

- 1997 *Stardust* (illustrated novel):

____

____

____

- 1999 *Stardust* (novel):

____

____

____

- 2007 *Stardust* (film):

____

____

____

2 What are the similarities and differences between them?

____

____

____

____

The fact that *Stardust* was originally an illustrated novel suggests that it is a visual tale, allowing it to be adapted to film effectively. When *Stardust* was first realised, Gaiman saw it as a postmodern fairy tale: 'I wanted to write a fairy tale and I wanted to write a story that felt like the kind of thing that they wrote before Tolkien.' In an interview, Gaiman commented, 'I wanted to write something where it was absolutely its own thing ... it was different, but it felt like a fantasy. It was always going to be a romance and I wanted it to be a romance ... even when I was writing it, I had the model of the old screwball comedies in my head. Sort of things like *It Happened One Night*, the idea of a couple on the road who hate each other that are going to end up eventually falling in love.'

Can a film adaptation ever be better than the book?

As you have probably experienced, debates about books and their film adaptations can be contentious. This is largely because reading is a personal experience. When we read, we imagine the scenes in our own unique way, which is usually not the same way as the filmmaker. This can often lead to disappointment when we eventually watch the adapted film. However, if we're not aware of the book, we will probably enjoy the film adaptation more.

In an interview about the film, Gaiman commented, 'It's very, very weird being the author of the book anyway, because, really, what you want for a film is for everyone to see it, you want everyone to love it, you want people to tell their friends, to go back again and come up to you on the street and say, "By the way, I saw your film, *Stardust*, and loved it and it was so moving and Michelle was so scary and De Niro was so funny and, oh my gosh, Charlie Cox, I loved it and I'm going to see it again and buy the DVD – but the book was better." And that's really what you want.'

Can a film adaptation surpass the original work, or will it inevitably play second fiddle?

2.5.5 Understanding and responding to texts A

The opening sequence

Stargazing [00:00:35 - 00:00:43]

1 The film opens with the voiceover of a narrator character, and the camera moves from the star and moon down along the telescope to reveal scientists at the Royal Academy of Science in London. Describe the camera movement and explain its effect.

2 The narrator says, 'A philosopher once asked, are we human because we gaze at the stars, or do we gaze at them because we are human? Pointless, really. Do the stars gaze back? Now, that's a question.' Explain what you think is the reason for this quotation as well as the setting. Does it add anything to the overall story or themes?

3 *Stardust* is meant to be a fairy tale. What elements of this genre did you notice?

Entering Stormhold [00:00:44 - 00:06:30]

4 How does Vaughn show that Stormhold is different from Dunstan's normal world of Victorian England?

Scan the QR code for additional content on music.

How well have the themes been rendered in the film?

Neil Gaiman, in talking about his book, said, '*Stardust*, for me, is about a boy becoming a man, and it's about that classic fairy tale thing of setting out to find something, to prove yourself. But it's also about that life thing – discovering that the thing you set out to find is very often not the thing you thought you were going to find. Going out on an adventure, whether in life or in fiction, changes you, and that for me was always the heart of *Stardust* when I was writing it. I wanted to write a story about a young man who sets out to find his heart's desire, and it wasn't what he thought it was. And what we've done with the film is compressed the story and squeezed it.'

We have seen that this theme has been 'squeezed' into the film and carried forward in the opening, when the narrator says, 'This is the story of how Tristan Thorn becomes a man, a much greater challenge altogether. For to achieve it, he must win the heart of his one true love.' This also touches on another key theme in the film: true love. The film presents the idea that we often lack insight when it comes to who our 'true' love is. What we actually want turns out to be what we least expect.

2.5.6 Reading, viewing and listening to texts

With a partner, brainstorm and discuss the themes you noticed in the film.

2.5.7 Understanding and responding to texts A

1 Watch some scenes and take notes about elements of Tristan's character development that communicate the theme of personal growth and love. You might like to look at some scenes like: Tristan's promise to Victoria; meeting Yvaine; seeing Victoria again; and running to the wall.

2 In the first column of the following table, make brief notes about the plot events. In the second column, take notes on the film techniques used. In the third column, analyse why they are used to communicate a theme. The first one has been done for you.

	What happens	How it happens	Why it happens
Meeting Tristan	We meet our hero with the 'unconventional heritage'. We learn that he seeks to win the heart of his true love. Tristan attempts to impress Victoria but is shown up (and beaten up!) by the charming Humphrey. Tristan is shown to be a not very skilful, suave or impressive hero.	The scene builds towards a pivotal moment of the two young lovers meeting (Romeo and Juliet style). The VO, music and dialogue build tension. This is then subverted when the low angle shot reveals Tristan and the disappointed reaction from Victoria. A low angle shot from Tristan's POV looking up at Humphrey makes Humphrey appear better and stronger than Tristan.	These scenes are designed to introduce the audience to Tristan and to reveal his character and qualities, and how he is not quite a 'man' yet. Because the scenes are shot from Tristan's perspective, the audience is positioned to empathise with and invest in the character.
Scene 2			
Scene 3			
Scene 4			

3 **The witches and their adventures to capture the star embody another theme in the film: eternal youth and beauty. How are the witches used to highlight this idea?**

4 'Why fight to be accepted by people you don't actually want to be like?' (Tristan Thorn)

A message in the film that could encapsulate all these themes is the importance of accepting who you are. Using your notes from the table, write a paragraph about how effectively the film communicates this message. Also, consider how context has influenced Vaughn in seeking to bring this message into the story.

2.5.8 Chapter reflection

1 Identify and explain one activity in this chapter that helped to inform and inspire your learning.

2 How has studying the film *Stardust* influenced your perception of film adaptations?

3 Let's return to the central inquiry question: ***How does film captivate audiences and provoke deeper thinking about themes and ideas?*** In this chapter, we have been evaluating the film's merits and how effectively it communicates the story of *Stardust*. You have been encouraged to consider the nature of film adaptations. One of our investigations was based on the extent to which a film adaptation can be better than the book. To bring your ideas together, let's think about the ending. Read the following quotation from Neil Gaiman:

... we changed the ending, which is something I knew we would have to do when I sold it to Miramax back in 1999. I loved, as an author, writing the end of the original novel because it's enormously fun, it's filled with lots of people missing each other and things that never hit in the way you expected them to. And it's sort of enormous fun for a reader, who is seeing everything from above and knows more about everything that's been happening than the characters do. But I realised even then it could be incredibly frustrating to have that ending happen if you were a viewer of a film, because you'll be sitting there and expect all these characters to meet at the end and then they all miss each other and you go, 'WHAT?! ...

4 To what extent would you agree with Gaiman's comment that the ending of the novel was 'enormously fun' but that he had to change it for the film? Reflect on how successful the changes were.

CHAPTER 6:

WILL THE REAL SHERLOCK HOLMES PLEASE STAND UP?

Chapter overview

In this chapter, you will explore the evolution of Sherlock Holmes in film. You will learn about the character's enduring popularity and how he was 'the man who never lived and will never die'.

You will examine how composers have sought to capture this super-sleuth through film over time.

Success criteria: In this chapter, I will be successful when I can ...

- draw on prior knowledge of texts to question, challenge and deepen understanding of both new and familiar texts
- analyse how contextual, creative and unconscious influences shape the composition, understanding and interpretation of all representations in films
- explore and analyse character representations in film and how they can reflect particular values.

Chapter inquiry questions

- Who is Sherlock Holmes?
- How have films represented Sherlock Holmes?
- How has Sherlock Holmes evolved over time?

Key vocabulary

- Palimpsest
- Sleuth
- Values

Who is Sherlock Holmes?

Meeting Sherlock

Before we delve into the many ways in which Sherlock has appeared in film, we need to meet the original hero.

Sherlock Holmes was created by Sir Arthur Conan Doyle in 1887. Holmes is an 'English consulting detective' who lives in London and is well known for his talent in solving mysteries using careful observation and sharp thinking. Holmes used innovative techniques like fingerprints, trace evidence and footprints to solve crimes long before the police started using them regularly. Doyle's stories helped introduce these methods to the world of crime-solving.

Sir Arthur Conan Doyle

Over a period of 40 years, Doyle created 56 short stories and four novels, mostly written from Dr Watson's point of view as he follows Holmes around and records the mysteries they solve together. These stories first appeared serialised in magazines, a common form of publication during the Victorian period.

Sherlock TV series co-creator Mark Gatiss commented that 'Over years and years of accumulating various versions and Victoriana, people had slightly lost sight of the fact that they're enormous fun! They're quick reads, they're jolly thrilling, blood-curdling thrilling adventures and really, that's what we wanted to do.'

Doyle's stories were first published in *The Strand Magazine*

2.6.1 Warm-up

'How did you know what I was doing? I believe you have eyes in the back of your head.' 'I have, at least, a well-polished, silver-plated coffee-pot in front of me,' said he. 'But, tell me, Watson, what do you make of our visitor's stick? Since we have been so unfortunate as to miss him and have no notion of his errand, this accidental souvenir becomes of importance. Let me hear you reconstruct the man by an examination of it.'

Sherlock Holmes: The Complete Novels and Stories Volume II, Sir Arthur Conan Doyle

Conduct a class discussion on how the characters 'reconstruct the man' and what it might mean.

Sherlock Holmes is one of the most recognisable figures in literature. Although Dracula is the most-played character of all time in movies and TV, the most-played human character is Sherlock Holmes. He is beloved from generation to generation and has been constantly renewed and reinterpreted in plays, films, radio, TV, comics and manga, and even computer games.

2.6.2 Reading, viewing and listening to texts

Scan the QR code to watch the video 'Who IS Sherlock Holmes'.

The video argues that the world of adaptation has made Holmes into a **palimpsest**:

'Sherlock is a cultural text, repeatedly altered over time as each new interpretation becomes superimposed over those that precede it. This means that Sherlock continually evolves, embodying ideas and **values** often far removed from those found in Conan Doyle. And, after each particular story ends, Sherlock rises again, a little changed, perhaps, with a new face and fresh mannerisms or turns of phrase, but still essentially Sherlock, our Sherlock.'

In critical theory, the word palimpsest is used metaphorically to describe the relationships texts have with each other – how newer texts relate to prior texts; the various ways a later text asks readers to read or remember an earlier one (e.g. parodies, pastiches, adaptations, transformations, allusions, etc.).

VOCABULARY

Palimpsest
noun: a written document, usually on vellum or parchment, that has been written upon several times, often with remnants of erased writing still visible.

Values
noun: beliefs or standards people have about what is right or wrong, what's important in life, that govern their behaviour or expectations.

1 Brainstorm a list of other examples of palimpsests. Share your ideas.

Sherlock Holmes made his debut in the novelette *A Study in Scarlet*.

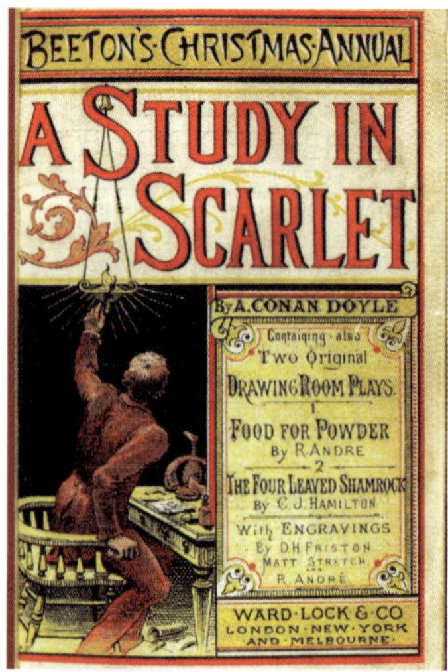

Holmes was loved and popular, but Doyle felt that 'I have had such an overdose of him that I feel towards him as I do towards paté de foie gras, of which I once ate too much, so that the name of it gives me a sickly feeling to this day.'

Doyle wanted to write 'serious' literature and be done with Holmes, so he decided to kill off his character in *The Final Problem*.

However, there was so much public outcry that Doyle was forced to resurrect the beloved detective. In an article published by the BBC, Jennifer Keishin Armstrong noted that 'The public reaction to the death was unlike anything previously seen for fictional events.'

There were some stories that 'young men throughout London wore black mourning crêpes on their hats or around their arms for the month of Holmes' death'. Furious readers wrote to the magazine calling Doyle a 'brute'! Americans started 'Let's Keep Holmes Alive' clubs.

How have films represented Sherlock Holmes?

The Adventures of Sherlock Holmes

Starring Basil Rathbone as Holmes and Nigel Bruce as Watson, and directed by Alfred L. Werker, this film, part of a series of Sherlock Holmes movies from the late 1930s and 1940s, was the first to become widely popular. In *The Adventures of Sherlock Holmes*, Holmes hunts his archenemy, Professor Moriarty, who is planning the crime of the century. Rathbone's portrayal is often regarded as one of the definitive depictions of Holmes.

The Adventures of Sherlock Holmes

Let's explore the film and see how the director sought to represent Holmes.

2.6.3 Reading, viewing and listening to texts

Using YouTube, watch the film trailer. As a class, describe what Sherlock Holmes is like in this film. Provide an example to support your observation.

Scan the QR code for additional activities.

2.6.4 Reading, viewing and listening to texts

In groups, search online and read Chapter I from *A Study in Scarlet* to learn about Doyle's Sherlock Holmes. This is the moment when Dr Watson and the reader meet Sherlock for the first time.

Chapter I. Mr. Sherlock Holmes.

IDENTIFY

Underline the details of the setting in the first two paragraphs. Discuss with a partner how the setting is preparing the reader for the character we are about to meet.

"But here we are, and you must form your own impressions about him." As [Stamford] spoke, we turned down a narrow lane and passed through a small side-door, which opened into [...] the chemical laboratory.

This was a lofty chamber, lined and littered with countless bottles. Broad, low tables were scattered about, which bristled with **retorts**, test-tubes, and little Bunsen lamps, with their blue flickering flames. There was only one student in the room, who was bending over a distant table absorbed in his work. At the sound of our steps he glanced round and sprang to his feet with a cry of pleasure. "I've found it! I've found it," he shouted to my companion, running towards us with a test-tube in his hand. "I have found a re-agent which is precipitated by haemoglobin, and by nothing else." [...]

"Dr. Watson, Mr. Sherlock Holmes," said Stamford, introducing us.

"How are you?" [Holmes] said cordially, gripping my hand with a strength for which I should hardly have given him credit. "You have been in Afghanistan, I perceive."

"How on earth did you know that?" I asked in astonishment.

"Never mind," said he, chuckling to himself. "The question now is about haemoglobin. No doubt you see the significance of this discovery of mine?"

"It is interesting, chemically, no doubt," I answered, "but practically—"

[He showed me his experiment.]

"Ha! ha!" he cried, clapping his hands, and looking as delighted as a child with a new toy. "What do you think of that?"

"It seems to be a very delicate test," I remarked. [...]

Stamford is a friend of both men and thinks they could move in together and share a flat.

VOCABULARY

Retort
noun: a vessel used for distillation of substances that are placed inside and subjected to heat.

“We came here on business,” said Stamford, sitting down on a high three-legged stool, and pushing another one in my direction with his foot. “My friend here wants to take **diggings**, and as you were complaining that you could get no one to go halves with you, I thought that I had better bring you together.”

> **VOCABULARY**
>
> **Diggings**
> *noun:* temporary accommodation.

Sherlock Holmes seemed delighted at the idea of sharing his rooms with me. “I have my eye on a suite in Baker Street,” he said, “which would suit us down to the ground. You don’t mind the smell of strong tobacco, I hope?”

“I always smoke ‘ship’s’ myself,” I answered.

“That’s good enough. I generally have chemicals about, and occasionally do experiments. Would that annoy you?”

“By no means.”

IDENTIFY

Highlight Sherlock Holmes’ ‘shortcomings’ the reader learns about in his conversation with Watson.

“Let me see—what are my other shortcomings. I get in the dumps at times, and don’t open my mouth for days on end. You must not think I am sulky when I do that. Just let me alone, and I’ll soon be right. What have you to confess now? It’s just as well for two fellows to know the worst of one another before they begin to live together.”

INTERPRET

Interpret what you think Holmes means when he says, ‘I get in the dumps at times, and don’t open my mouth for days on end. You must not think I am sulky when I do that. Just let me alone, and I’ll soon be right.’

I laughed at this cross-examination. “I keep a bull pup,” I said, “and I object to rows because my nerves are shaken, and I get up at all sorts of ungodly hours, and I am extremely lazy. [...]

[He cried, with a merry laugh,] “I think we may consider the thing as settled —that is, if the rooms are agreeable to you.”

“When shall we see them?”

“Call for me here at noon to-morrow, and we’ll go together and settle everything,” he answered.

“All right—noon exactly,” said I, shaking his hand.

We left him working among his chemicals, and we walked together towards my hotel.

“By the way,” I asked suddenly, stopping and turning upon Stamford, “how the deuce did he know that I had come from Afghanistan?”

My companion smiled an enigmatical smile. “That’s just his little **peculiarity**,” he said. “A good many people have wanted to know how he finds things out.”

> **VOCABULARY**
>
> **peculiarity**
> *noun:* a strange or unusual feature or habit.

“Oh! a mystery is it?” I cried, rubbing my hands. [...] “Good-bye,” I [said], and strolled on to my hotel, considerably interested in my new acquaintance.

Chapter II. The Science of Deduction.

Consider what Sherlock Holmes is like.

How does Watson respond to Holmes?

We met next day as he had arranged, and inspected the rooms at No. 221b, Baker Street, of which he had spoken at our meeting. [...]

Holmes was certainly not a difficult man to live with. He was quiet in his ways, and his habits were regular. It was rare for him to be up after ten at night [...]. Sometimes he spent his day at the chemical laboratory, sometimes in the dissecting-rooms, and occasionally in long walks [...]. On [some] occasions I have noticed such a dreamy, vacant expression in his eyes, that I might have suspected him of being addicted to the use of some narcotic [...].

IDENTIFY

Re-read the extracts and identify the words and phrases that describe Holmes (pay attention to the verbs and adjectives).

1 Compare Doyle's representation of Holmes with Werker's. Discuss what was surprising, different or contradictory. Record your discussion below.

2 Outline the characteristics of Holmes that Werker has maintained and carried forward into the film.

Scan the QR code for additional activities.

How has Sherlock Holmes evolved over time?

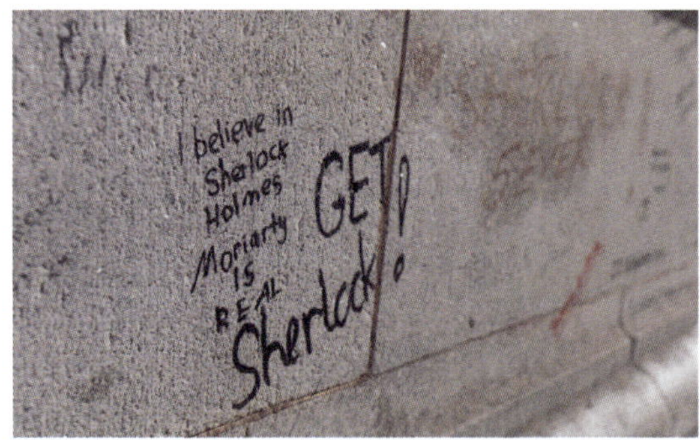

Amazingly, not only has intense and devoted following of Sherlock Holmes continued, but fans have only become more obsessive. Over the last 120 years, we have seen Sherlock Holmes' popularity grow exponentially and, with it, a constant stream of reimaginings. The detective has appeared in more than 260 films.

We are now going to examine the character development of Sherlock Holmes across two films and analyse whether the character evolves or remains consistent.

Scan the QR code for additional content and activities.

Sherlock Holmes

Even though there have been many Sherlock Holmes films since *The Adventures of Sherlock Holmes*, the next significant and hugely popular one did not occur until 2009. The plot of this film is rather traditional: Sherlock Holmes and his stalwart partner Watson engage in a battle of wits and brawn with a nemesis whose plot is a threat to all of England. However, what is not traditional is how the director, Guy Ritchie, brought a dynamic and action-oriented interpretation to the classic detective duo. *Sherlock Holmes* stars two famous actors, Robert Downey Jr. as Sherlock Holmes and Jude Law as Dr John Watson. This was a very interesting casting choice and rather controversial due to Downey's unconventional and more 'modern' depiction of Holmes.

2.6.5 Reading, viewing and listening to texts

Let's examine the film and see how the director has sought to represent Holmes.

1 Using YouTube, watch the film trailer.

2 Describe what Sherlock Holmes is like in this film. Provide an example to support your answer.

Enola Holmes

We now come to another film representation, *Enola Holmes*, directed by Harry Bradbeer. While not a traditional Sherlock Holmes film, this movie features Henry Cavill as an older and more caring Sherlock. The story primarily revolves around his younger sister, Enola Holmes, played by Millie Bobby Brown. When Enola discovers her mother is missing, she endeavours to find her, becoming a super-sleuth in her own right as she outwits her famous brother and unravels a dangerous conspiracy.

2.6.6 Reading, viewing and listening to texts

Let's examine the film and see how the director has sought to represent Holmes.

1 Predict what you think the characters of Enola and Sherlock will be like in the film.

2 Using YouTube, watch the film trailer.

3 Discuss with a partner what you think of this transformation of the stories of Sherlock Holmes.

Scan the QR code for additional content and activities.

2.6.7 Chapter reflection

1 Outline two things you will remember about Sherlock Holmes.

2 After viewing some of the film depictions of Sherlock Holmes, what are the common traits and characteristics that persist?

3 How has studying multiple representations of Sherlock Holmes influenced your perception of the character and the stories?

4 Let's return to the central inquiry question: ***How does film captivate audiences and provoke deeper thinking about themes and ideas?*** This chapter has encouraged you to understand how film is a powerful medium as it can reach many audiences, influencing them to respond to characters, ideas and values in a particular way. Reflect on personal experiences with films that have had a lasting impact on your thoughts, beliefs or perspectives. How did these films engage you intellectually or emotionally, and what aspects of the storytelling contributed to their influential power?

Unit 2: **Summative assessment**

The summative assessment options below provide opportunities to demonstrate your achievement of the following outcomes and focus areas.

Outcome and focus area	**EN5-RVL-01** **Reading, viewing and listening to texts**	**EN5-URA-01** **Understanding and responding to texts A**	**EN5-URB-01** **Understanding and responding to texts B**	**EN5-ECA-01** **Expressing ideas and composing texts A**	**EN5-ECB-01** **Expressing ideas and composing texts B**
Content point	Reading, viewing and listening for meaning	Representation	Theme	Speaking	Planning, monitoring and revising
		Characterisation		Text features	Reflecting
	Reflecting		Argument and authority		

Option 1: Mugatu monologue

Mugatu, in the film *Zoolander*, is the stereotype of a fashion designer. He is also the antagonist who is greedy and immoral, demonstrated through his exploitation of children for cheap labour in Malaysia. Stiller creates him to criticise the greedy, corrupt and superficial nature of the fashion industry.

Write a monologue from Mugatu's perspective.

Demonstrate how satire can help audiences to question particular values and attitudes about their world (such as fast fashion, sustainability or the nature of the celebrity). To help illustrate and support your ideas, use details from the film studied in this unit and other examples of your own choosing to satirise Mugatu's perspective on the fashion industry and his attitude towards beauty.

Create a plan to demonstrate the sequence of your argument. Outline your thesis and supporting points, as well as the topic for each paragraph. Submit your plan for feedback and use the feedback to revise your final submission.

Present your monologue to the class.

Be guided by the following questions when planning, writing and producing your monologue.

- What argument do you want to make about the fashion industry, superficiality and ideas of beauty?
- How has the film represented the character Mugatu? How does the representation reflect the values and attitudes of its time?
- How will you represent the character Mugatu? How will your representation reflect the values and attitudes of your time?
- Who is your audience and what is your purpose?
- Which rhetorical strategies can you use to position your audience and evoke an emotional response?
- How can you use the structural conventions of persuasive texts to purposefully justify opinions and develop expanding arguments (e.g. a focused opening and thesis, logically sequenced elaboration paragraphs, and a conclusion that synthesises complex ideas)?

Option 2: Discursive response

In Chapter 5 we examined the question 'Can a film adaptation ever be better than the book?' and you have explored how this is a rather contentious topic with strong opinions on either side of the debate.

With reference to a book and its film adaptation of your own choosing, compose a discursive response.

Reflect on what you learnt in Chapter 5 about the nature of film adaptations and your own opinions on this question.

Create a plan to demonstrate the sequence of your ideas. Outline your thesis and supporting points, as well as the topic for each paragraph. Submit your plan for feedback and use the feedback to revise your final submission.

Be guided by the following questions when planning, writing and producing your composition.

- What book and film adaptation will you use for your composition?
- What is your opinion: is the book or film better? Or, do you think one is more nuanced? Outline your opinion in one sentence.
- Identify the changes made from the book to the film. Did they enhance or detract from the enjoyment of the story, characters or ideas?
- What are the challenges involved in adapting a book to film?
- How well have the themes from the book been rendered in the film?
- Who is your audience and what is your purpose?
- Which **rhetorical strategies** can you use to position your audience and evoke an emotional response?
- How can you use structure to purposefully justify opinions and develop expanding arguments (e.g. a focused opening and thesis, logically sequenced elaboration paragraphs, and a conclusion that synthesises complex ideas)?

Option 3: Persuasive speech

> The obvious reason for Holmes' enduring appeal is that, while he possesses no superpowers – his parents weren't wizards, no radioactive spider bit him – his gifts are cool enough to be superhuman. Playing to our fantasies of being smarter than everyone else, Holmes performs jaw-dropping feats of perception.
>
> (*Sherlock: A Character Who's More than Elementary*, John Powers)

The Sherlock Holmes Society of London has asked you to be the keynote speaker at their next annual conference.

Compose a persuasive speech that explores the 'enduring appeal' of Sherlock Holmes. Reflect on what you learnt in Chapter 6 about Sherlock Holmes and your own opinions on his evolution through film.

Create a plan to demonstrate the sequence of your argument. Outline your thesis and supporting points, as well as the topic for each paragraph. Submit your plan for feedback and use the feedback to revise your final submission.

Present your speech to the class.

Be guided by the following questions when planning, writing and producing your speech.

- How have the film representations of Sherlock Holmes captured his **character** and his appeal?
- How does each representation of Sherlock Holmes reflect the **values** and attitudes of its time?
- Does Sherlock Holmes have an **enduring relevance**?
- Who is your audience and what is your purpose?
- Which **rhetorical strategies** can you use to position your audience and evoke an emotional response?
- How can you use the structural conventions of persuasive texts to purposefully justify opinions and develop expanding arguments (e.g. a focused opening and thesis, logically sequenced elaboration paragraphs, and a conclusion that synthesises complex ideas)?

Assessment as learning: self-assessment

Does my composition:

- ☐ present a clear argument?
- ☐ use appropriate structure?
- ☐ experiment with rhetorical strategies and structure?
- ☐ craft concise sentences?

How effectively did my plan and drafts help me to draft and revise my composition?

____

____

____

What are two strengths of my response?

____

____

What area/s of my response do I need to refine further?

____

____

UNIT 03

Artistry in poetry

Unit inquiry question:
Is poetry 'simply the best words in the best order'?

Students will analyse the ideas and stylistic features of poetry of all different forms and modes. They will consider how personal, social and historical context shapes the perspective of the poet and can educate a reader as to the central concerns of the day.

Through reading and reflecting on a range of poetry, students will develop a deeper understanding of how ideas are conveyed by the persona through ambitious language forms and features. They will do this through an in-depth study of a single poet.

This unit has been broken into three chapters, which each look at a different aspect of texts and the world and raise additional inquiry questions.

Chapter 7

'A sentence starts out like a lone traveler …'

This chapter examines the intriguing, funny and thought-provoking poetry of American poet Billy Collins. Through his often unique perspective, students will explore the what, how and why of his poetry.

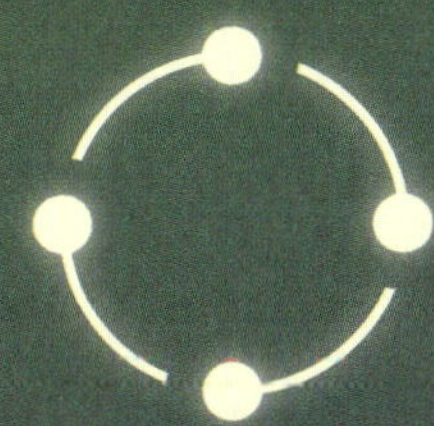

Chapter 8

Romanticism – love, nature and revolution

This chapter will lead students in their understanding of the Romantic movement, considering not only how it was so different from what went before it, but also its legacy.

Chapter 9

Love poetry – a match made in heaven?

This chapter explores how the universal emotion of love has been represented in poetry throughout the ages and continues to be a popular subject for poets and lyricists in the twenty-first century.

The learning activities within each chapter and the summative assessment options (on pages 125–127) provide opportunities to assess student achievement of the following outcomes.

Outcome and focus area	Content point
EN5-RVL-01 Reading, viewing and listening to texts	**Reading, viewing and listening for meaning**
	Analyse how the use of language forms and features in texts have the capacity to create multiple meanings
EN5-URA-01 Understanding and responding to texts A	**Code and convention**
	Use metalanguage effectively to analyse how meaning is constructed by linguistic and stylistic elements in texts
	Connotation, imagery and symbol
	Analyse how figurative language and devices can be used to represent complex ideas, thoughts and feelings to contribute to larger patterns of meaning in texts, and experiment with this in own texts
EN5-URB-01 Understanding and responding to texts B	**Perspective and context**
	Analyse how elements of an author's personal, cultural and political contexts can shape their perspectives and representation of ideas, including form and purpose
	Appreciate how all communication is a product of cultural context
	Argument and authority
	Analyse how an engaging personal voice in texts can represent a perspective or argument and communicate a sense of authority, and experiment with these ideas in own texts
	Research, select and sequence appropriate evidence from texts and reliable sources to construct cohesive and authoritative arguments
	Style
	Analyse how the distinctive aesthetic qualities and stylistic features of a text can shape and be shaped by its purpose, and experiment with this in own texts
	Examine the way an author's distinct personal style shapes meaning in their work
	Appreciate how the style of a text can represent larger ideas of literary movements and genres

EN5-ECA-01	**Writing**
Expressing ideas and composing texts A	Develop a personal and informed voice that generates ideas and positions an audience through selection of appropriate word-level language and text-level features
	Experiment with language to create tone, atmosphere and mood
	Speaking
	Craft a range of spoken, signed or communicated texts that convey complex ideas for specific audiences
	Signal the development of ideas through language, structure and presentational features
	Text features
	Experiment with a range of poetic forms to explore ideas and express personal perspectives
	Experiment with a combination of modes for specific effect and impact

CHAPTER 7:

'A SENTENCE STARTS OUT LIKE A LONE TRAVELER …'

Chapter overview

In this chapter, you will investigate the life and times of the poet Billy Collins and how his context and experiences might have influenced his writing. You will find out who or what influences him in writing his poems and think about how you can see this manifested in them. You will reflect on their part in a wider timeline of American poets.

Success criteria: In this chapter, I will be successful when I can …

- appreciate how the use of language can have the capacity to create multiple meanings
- analyse how aspects of an author's context can influence their perspective
- analyse how an engaging persona can influence the reader's understanding of authority in a poem
- analyse how figurative language and devices can be used to show a range of thoughts and emotions
- experiment with a range of poetic forms, figurative language and devices to explore ideas
- make vocabulary choices which enhance stylistic features of my writing and shape meaning.

Chapter inquiry questions

- How can context contribute to our understanding of a poet's work?
- How does Collins transform an ordinary human experience into something extraordinary?
- How does Collins use language features, including symbols and motifs, to convey humour in his poetry?
- What universal themes are explored in the poetry of Collins?

Key vocabulary

- Context
- Persona
- Tone
- Allusion

Billy Collins

Billy Collins

American poet Billy Collins is famous for his conversational, witty poems which often begin with humour and end with poignancy or a tender, profound observation.

Collins himself said, 'I have one reader in mind, someone who is in the room with me, and who I'm talking to, and I want to make sure I don't talk too fast, or too glibly. Usually, I try to create a hospitable tone at the beginning of a poem. Stepping from the title to the first lines is like stepping into a canoe. A lot of things can go wrong.'

3.7.1 Warm-up

Read the poem titled 'Embrace' by Billy Collins.

You know the parlor trick.
Wrap your arms around your own body
and from the back it looks like
someone is embracing you,
her hands grasping your shirt,
her fingernails teasing your neck.

From the front it is another story.
You never looked so alone,
your crossed elbows and screwy grin.
You could be waiting for a tailor
to fit you for a straitjacket,
one that would hold you really tight.

This poem is about how we can interpret the same action in different ways, depending on where we place ourselves.

It comes from a collection titled *The Apple that Astonished Paris*. Here, Collins has appropriated a famous quotation by French painter Paul Cezanne – by it, Cezanne means he would use an ordinary object, like an apple, to create new meaning. How does this poem take an ordinary action to create new meaning for the reader?

____

____

____

How can context contribute to our understanding of a poet's work?

Where and when a writer or artist grew up, who they were friends with or what was happening at the time they were working, can all influence their work. For instance, jazz music, with its improvisational and free-form qualities, had a significant impact on the 'beat generation' of poets in the 1940s and 1950s.

3.7.2 Understanding and responding to texts B

1 In groups, research the life and times of Billy Collins. As you do, think about the people, places, music and ideas that influenced him and shaped his poetry.

Write down what you learn from your research about:

- Collins' life – his family, growing up, education
- who or what or where has influenced his poetry
- his famous poems and any accolades he has received
- what his attitude is towards poetry and the craft of writing
- anything else you discover that is interesting, unusual or amusing.

In your group, share what you have learned.

2 Choose the most valuable pieces of information from your research, then choose an object that you think could represent what you have discovered about Billy Collins.

- Find the physical object or an image of it and explain why it is important in understanding the life and times of Billy Collins. For instance, he was a great jazz fan and uses lots of musical metaphors in his poetry, so one object might be an instrument or a jazz record.
- As a group, present your objects to the class – making clear the link to Billy Collins, his life or his poetry.
- Finish your presentation by answering the inquiry question: ***How can context contribute to our understanding of the poet's work***?

How does Billy Collins transform an ordinary human experience into something extraordinary?

Poets can communicate ideas about the significance of everyday experiences, but they can also delve deeper into ideas and experiences.

Billy Collins' poetry is often amusing because he can explore a single experience and reflect on it in a humorous, sometimes unusual, way. One poem that does this is titled 'Another Reason Why I Don't Keep a Gun in the House'.

3.7.3 Reading, viewing and listening to texts

Find the poem online and read it. As a class, discuss the following.

1 What is the single human experience that has provoked this poem?

2 At the end of the first stanza, the poet uses a metaphor comparing the dog to a light switch. Discuss with a partner why this is an effective image.

3 After the second stanza, the poet uses this common human experience to move from reality to imagination. What is the new image of the dog the reader is presented with?

3.7.4 Understanding and responding to texts A

1 Explain how the repetition escalates the persona's impatience as the reader continues through the poem.

2 How does the image of the dog change throughout the poem and how is this designed to amuse the reader?

3 The poet uses humour to transform an irritating experience into one that is absurd but amusing. Write an analytical paragraph to explain how he does this. Try using the PETAL structure to help you organise your thinking.

3.7.5 Expressing ideas and composing texts A

Over to you ...

Think of an ordinary object or moment. Compose a poem that begins with this moment, but as the poem progresses transform it into something extraordinary or absurd.

Here is a suggestion to get you started.

Ordinary event that starts the poem	Extraordinary transformation
Putting on your socks in the morning	The socks have transformed into snakes or eels trying to imprison you to prevent you from going to school.

How does Collins use language features, including symbols and motifs, to convey humour in his poetry?

Poetic devices such as metaphor, simile and symbols are essential tools of most poets, who use a range of stylistic features to express complex emotions and ideas in vivid and tangible ways. Figurative language can transport readers into the emotional and sensory world of the poem.

Poets desire to organise the 'best words in the best order' and figurative language allows them to do this.

3.7.6 Understanding and responding to texts A

Read the following extracts from Collins' poems below. Highlight the figurative language in each one and write underneath which TWO things are being compared.

Extract 1

I can hear the library humming in the night,
a choir of authors murmuring inside their books [from 'Books' by Billy Collins]

Extract 2

A sentence starts out like a lone traveler
heading into a blizzard at midnight [from 'Winter Syntax' by Billy Collins]

Extract 3

... the memories you used to harbor
decided to retire to the southern hemisphere of the brain,
to a little fishing village where there are no phones [from 'Forgetfulness' by Billy Collins]

3.7.7 Reading, viewing and listening to texts

Symbols and motifs can often draw attention to significant ideas in poems, guiding the reader in their interpretation. They can allow the poet to approach familiar things in original and inventive ways, like when Collins uses the symbol of the orchestra to distract the persona from the annoyance of the barking dog.

In his poem 'Sweet Talk', Collins uses the **motif** of art and the **symbol** of sunlight to express love for another.

Listen to/watch it using the QR code.

3.7.8 Understanding and responding to texts A

1 Write down the line/s that draw attention to the symbol of sunlight. Why do you think this is an effective **symbol** to reflect the idea of love?

2 In the poem, four artists or artworks are referred to.

You can see images of them clearly in the video. Discuss with a friend what you think the images of the Mona Lisa, Venus and Delacroix's painting all have in common? Write your thoughts below.

____

____

____

____

3 When a symbol is used repeatedly in a poem it can be called a **motif**. Why do you think that Collins used the motif of **art** in this poem? How does it represent his perspective on love?

____

____

____

____

Motifs can symbolise the same thing throughout a single poem, but sometimes their meaning can change or evolve throughout. Collins also use motifs in a humorous way. In his poems 'The Country' and 'Mice', he uses a mouse to convey different things.

In 'Mice' the rodent begins as symbol of a lonely childhood:

> so many hours I would watch
> your comings and goings,
> before someone called me down to dinner

But at the end of the poem, the poet presents the reader with an amusing image of the persona as an old man, using the mouse as a symbol of friendship and familiarity, 'full of oatmeal and a mouse on my shoulder, / standing on its hind legs, whispering in my ear.'

The persona of 'The Country' imagines mice setting fire to the house he is staying in. He speaks of the mice as mischievous and inventive, which is engaging for the reader, making them smile at the absurdity of the persona's imagination.

3.7.9 Reading, viewing and listening to texts

1 Read the poem 'The Country' and think about how the poet uses stylistic features to engage you.

You will see that some words/phrases have been highlighted to get you started – identify each feature used here and write an annotation explaining why it is effective.

The Country

I wondered about you
when you told me never to leave
a box of wooden, strike-anywhere matches
lying around the house because the mice

might get into them and start a fire.
But your face was absolutely straight
when you twisted the lid down on the round tin
where the matches, you said, are always stowed.

Who could sleep that night?
Who could whisk away the thought
of the one unlikely mouse
padding along a cold water pipe

behind the floral wallpaper
gripping a single wooden match
between the needles of his teeth?
Who could not see him rounding a corner,

the blue tip scratching against a rough-hewn beam,
the sudden flare, and the creature
for one bright, shining moment
suddenly thrust ahead of his time –

now a fire-starter, now a torch-bearer
in a forgotten ritual, little brown druid
illuminating some ancient night.
Who could fail to notice,

lit up in the blazing insulation,
the tiny looks of wonderment on the faces
of his fellow mice, one-time inhabitants
of what once was our house in the country?

Scan the QR code to watch the animated representation of 'The Country'.

2 How has watching this interpretation of the poem enriched or changed your understanding of it?

____

____

____

____

____

____

You will have noticed some characteristics of Billy Collins' poetry, such as common use of the pronouns 'I' and 'you' to establish the connection between himself as poet, the persona and the reader, and including animals doing unusual things to create humour.

Another characteristic of his poetry is the inclusion of **allusions** to places and famous people, sometimes historical, to create unusual comparisons between them and the subject or ideas of the poem.

VOCABULARY

Allusion
noun: reference within the text to something beyond the text, to create layers of meaning, add humour or even establish and consolidate a particular tone.

What universal themes are explored in the poetry of Billy Collins?

3.7.10 Understanding and responding to texts C

Group activity:

Below is a list of some of Collins' poems, grouped around central **themes**.

Get into groups and choose a theme from those listed.

Read the suggested poems as a starting point, but if you like Collins' poetry see if you can dive deeper and find some extra examples.

Language and poetry

- Introduction to Poetry
- The Trouble with Poetry
- Aristotle

Aging

- On Turning Ten
- The Man in the Moon
- Forgetfulness

Books and learning

- Schoolsville
- Marginalia
- Books

Art and creativity

- Winter Syntax
- Aristotle
- Budapest

Your task:

- Access each of these poems via the internet and read them all carefully.
- Discuss with your group how Collins has represented the theme in the poems you have read.
- Discuss how the representation of the theme has value in today's context.
- Identify a few lines from each poem that show how he has done this by 'exploding the quote' (see below).

How to 'explode the quote'.

The poem 'Schoolsville' has a universal theme of the past, represented in the quotation:

> Glancing over my shoulder at the past,
> I realise the number of students I have taught
> Is enough to populate a small town.
> I can see it nestled in a paper landscape,
> chalk dust flurrying down in winter,
> nights dark as a blackboard.

To explode this part of the poem to show how the theme of the past is represented, take ONE element – a metaphor, a symbol, a rhetorical device, etc. – and show the connection between language and theme.

For instance:

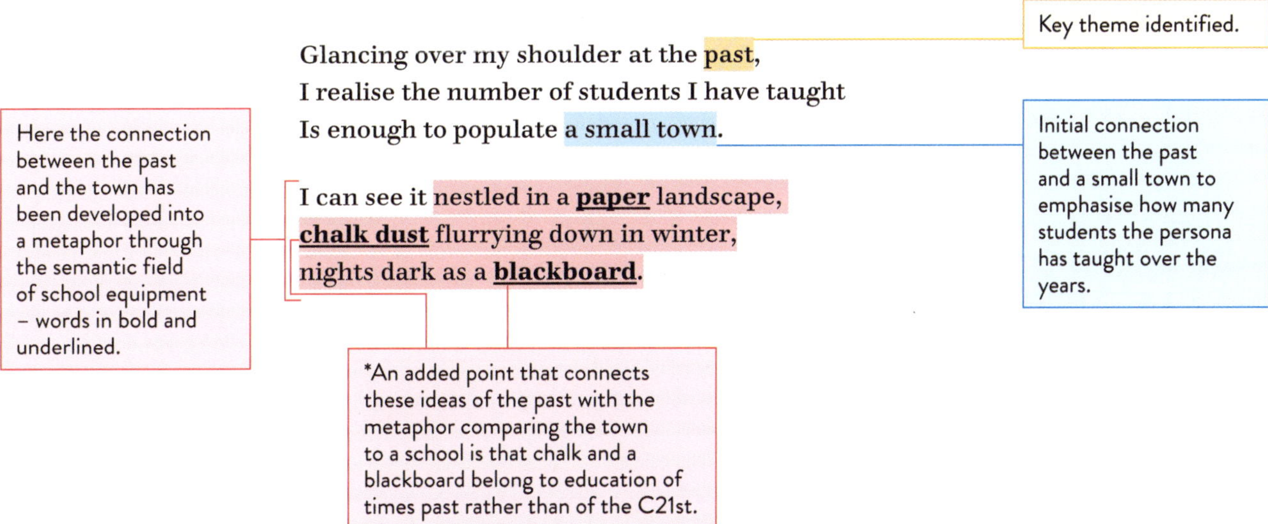

Then consider, in the light of this metaphor, how and why the images of students/school connect to the past. You could even reflect on the significance of the title of the poem.

3.7.11 Chapter reflection

1 Poetry can often be challenging at best and incomprehensible at worst. Billy Collins said that he tries 'to create a hospitable tone at the beginning of a poem'. Do you think he succeeds in this? Try to give some examples from the poems you have read.

2 In this chapter you have investigated structure and language in Collins' poetry, both of which he uses in unexpected ways. Reflect on where he has done this; cite the example you found most interesting and explain why.

3 Let's return to the central inquiry question: ***Is poetry 'simply the best words in the best order'?***

Discuss this with a peer in light of Billy Collins' poetry. Where does this perspective seem to align with his work? Do you agree that this is the essence of what poetry is?

CHAPTER 8:

ROMANTICISM – LOVE, NATURE AND REVOLUTION

Chapter overview

In this chapter, you will learn about Romanticism, a movement that emerged at the end of the eighteenth century from the work of philosophers Jean-Jacques Rousseau and Edmund Burke, and German poet and novelist Johann Wolfgang von Goethe.

In this chapter, you will explore the ways in which the poets of the Romantic movement embraced their artistic creativity in language and style, described their connections with the world, and articulated their thoughts and feelings in their personal expression.

Success criteria: In this chapter, I will be successful when I can ...

- express in spoken and written communication a clear understanding of the context and culture of Romanticism and its legacy
- identify and compare the stylistic features of different Romantic poets and paintings
- clearly communicate complex ideas and information to my peers.

Chapter inquiry questions

- What is Romanticism?
- How does Romanticism reflect the cultural shifts and societal changes of the time?
- How do Romantic poets share certain stylistic characteristics while maintaining their individual voices?
- What has been the lasting impact of Romanticism?

Key vocabulary

- Sensibility
- Sublime
- Subjectivity
- Imagination

What is Romanticism?

Romanticism, a literary movement from the late eighteenth to mid-nineteenth centuries, was a rebellion against strict rules of the past.

Imagine a group of creative rebels who cherished **emotions**, individuality and nature's beauty. Romantic writers painted vivid pictures with words, exploring intense feelings, personal experiences, and the awe-inspiring wonders of the natural world.

They believed in the power of **imagination** to express unique perspectives, challenging traditional ideas. Romanticism celebrated the heart over the mind, encouraging dreamers to find beauty in life's complexities, and influencing poetry, novels and art with a spirit of passion, freedom and a touch of the extraordinary.

Romantic writers and artists believed in the importance of the experience of the individual and this was a driving force behind the perspectives offered in their work. This allowed their work to be personal, or **subjective**, rather than objective, creating for the reader an intimate understanding and appreciation of the Romantic mind.

In the context of Romanticism, **sensibility** refers to a heightened emotional responsiveness and an acute awareness of one's own feelings and the feelings of others. It is closely linked to the emphasis on emotions, subjectivity and individual experience that characterised the Romantic movement.

3.8.1 Warm-up

You are a modern-day Romantic concerned with your **emotions**, your **imagination** and your **relationship to your natural world**, whether that is in the country, town or city.

In the pie chart below, brainstorm the ideas that stem from these concerns.

emotions

relationship to your natural world

imagination

3.8.2 Reading, viewing and listening to texts

When the Romantics had an experience that was awe-inspiring or overwhelming, they used the word **sublime**. To these thinkers, the sublime was a feeling or vision that elicited both fascination and fear.

1 Look carefully at the paintings below, painted by Romantic artists famous for their depictions of the sublime.

The Slave Ship by J. M. W. Turner

Scan the QR codes to read a bit more about these paintings.

Wanderer above the Sea of Fog by Caspar David Friedrich

2 After reading and discussing in a small group, write down three bullet points that illustrate how each of these paintings conveys the Romantic ideal of the sublime.

- Remember to use your knowledge of visual techniques in your discussions.
- Colour code ideas that are similar/different.

The Slave Ship conveys the Romantic ideal of the sublime because ...	*Wanderer above the Sea of Fog* conveys the Romantic ideal of the sublime because ...
1	1
2	2
3	3

How does Romanticism reflect the cultural shifts and societal changes of the time?

The eighteenth century signified the **Age of Enlightenment** in which people centred the pursuit of knowledge on science and reason, and explored disciplines of the law, government and the separation of church and state. The writing of the Enlightenment is characterised by adhering to classical language, forms and allusions, using satire and wit to highlight intellectual inquiry and comment on the political, social or cultural times.

Romanticism was, in part, a reaction *against* the rationalism and scientific focus of the Enlightenment. It rejected strict logic and order by embracing emotion, intuition and the place of the individual and the imagination.

3.8.3 Understanding and responding to texts A

In the following two poetic extracts, Alexander Pope satirises his society's preoccupation with physical appearance by exaggerating how a woman's 'locks' or hair might be a reason to destroy mankind; his focus is logical reasoning through satire. On the other hand, as a Romantic poet, William Wordsworth describes his personal, emotional experience in a natural setting.

Each of these extracts uses the strict poetic form **iambic pentameter**. Look this up and write your findings below.

The first extract also uses **heroic couplets**. Look these up and write your findings below.

Discussion activity

Read the following extracts of poetry.

In pairs, discuss two differences in style between them.

Extract 1: from 'The Rape of the Lock' by Alexander Pope, a poet of the Enlightenment

This Nymph, to the destruction of mankind,
Nourish'd two Locks, which graceful hung behind
In equal curls, and well conspir'd to deck
With shining ringlets the smooth iv'ry neck.

Circle the word/s in extract 1 that indicate a classical reference.

Extract 2: from 'Lines Composed a Few Miles Above Tintern Abbey' by William Wordsworth, a Romantic poet

In each extract, indicate what the rhyme scheme is (e.g. ABAB).

Five years have passed; five summers, with the length
Of five long winters! and again I hear
These waters, rolling from their mountain-springs
With a soft inland murmur.

In extract 2, circle the pronoun that indicates the persona is concerned with their own thoughts and feelings.

1 How does the structure of the poetry aid its flow?

2 Which of these extracts do you find easier to understand and/or connect with? Justify your thinking.

Let's delve into context ...

In the nineteenth century, there were many changes afoot, both in England and overseas, that had a significant impact on the artists and writers of the day. The outbreak of the **French Revolution** ignited hope of change and great expectations of a fairer world, but the sweep of terror that ensued shattered this optimism for many.

The **Industrial Revolution** led to significant societal changes, including urbanisation and the rise of factories. International struggles, such as the French Revolution, in which ordinary people were fighting for freedom from the rule of the aristocracy, influenced Romantics. They often idealised rural life and nature, expressing nostalgia for a simpler, pre-industrialised era, when society was underpinned by freedom for the working man.

William Blake (1757–1827) was a famous early Romantic poet, painter and printmaker. He had a strong social conscience and highlighted the hardships of ordinary working people, particularly children, in his poetry.

In his poem 'The Chimney Sweeper', the reader can see his revolutionary views. This poem exposes the awful conditions of the boys known as climbing boys, whose work hours were long and whose task was dangerous. The persona of the poem embodies the voice of a young chimney sweeper, presumably six or seven years old.

3.8.4 Reading, viewing and listening to texts

Read the poem below – silently first and then aloud with a partner, taking turns, verse by verse.

The Chimney Sweeper

by William Blake

When my mother died I was very young,
And my father sold me while yet my tongue
Could scarcely cry " 'weep! 'weep! 'weep! 'weep!"
So your chimneys I sweep & in soot I sleep.

There's little Tom Dacre, who cried when his head
That curled like a lamb's back, was shaved, so I said,
"Hush, Tom! never mind it, for when your head's bare,
You know that the soot cannot spoil your white hair."

And so he was quiet, & that very night,
As Tom was a-sleeping he had such a sight!
That thousands of sweepers, Dick, Joe, Ned, & Jack,
Were all of them locked up in coffins of black;

And by came an Angel who had a bright key,
And he opened the coffins & set them all free;
Then down a green plain, leaping, laughing they run,
And wash in a river and shine in the Sun.

Then naked & white, all their bags left behind,
They rise upon clouds, and sport in the wind.
And the Angel told Tom, if he'd be a good boy,
He'd have God for his father & never want joy.

And so Tom awoke; and we rose in the dark
And got with our bags & our brushes to work.
Though the morning was cold, Tom was happy & warm;
So if all do their duty, they need not fear harm.

Show your understanding of the poem by answering the following questions. Each number correlates to a stanza in the poem.

Highlight the words/phrases that provide evidence for your thinking.

1 **What does the reader learn about the lives of children in the nineteenth century?**

2 **What does Blake communicate about the character of the chimney sweeper?**

3 **What structural feature is Blake using here to sustain the poem's pace?**

4 and **5** Tom has a dream – what does he dream about? What do you think Blake is trying to communicate here about the life of a chimney sweeper?

6 **In the final stanza, what consolation does Blake offer the boys?**

How do Romantic poets share certain stylistic characteristics while maintaining their individual voices?

William Blake was not only critical of the conditions of the working poor, but also wrote of the way that industrialisation had a negative impact on the natural environment. He saw that urban living often left people dehumanised and struggling to see beauty in the world.

In contrast, his contemporary, William Wordsworth, was inspired by nature and saw a divine beauty in it. Wordsworth, who lived in the Lake District – a particularly spectacular part of England – was able to see beauty even in urban environments.

Both poets are considered to be the forerunners of English Romanticism and share many stylistic characteristics in their use of metaphorical language, rhyme and rhythm.

3.8.5 Reading, viewing and listening to texts

Read the following two poems, both about London at the turn of the nineteenth century. They offer very different perspectives of the city.

London

by William Blake

I wander thro' each charter'd street,
Near where the charter'd Thames does flow.
And mark in every face I meet
Marks of weakness, marks of woe.

In every cry of every Man,
In every Infant's cry of fear,
In every voice: in every ban,
The mind-forg'd manacles I hear

How the Chimney-sweeper's cry
Every blackning Church appalls,
And the hapless Soldier's sigh
Runs in blood down Palace walls.

But most thro' midnight streets I hear
How the youthful Harlot's curse
Blasts the new-born Infant's tear
And blights with plagues the Marriage hearse.

Lines Composed upon Westminster Bridge

by William Wordsworth

Earth has not any thing to show more fair:
Dull would he be of soul who could pass by
A sight so touching in its majesty:
This City now doth, like a garment, wear
The beauty of the morning; silent, bare,
Ships, towers, domes, theatres, and temples lie
Open unto the fields, and to the sky;
All bright and glittering in the smokeless air.
Never did sun more beautifully steep
In his first splendour, valley, rock, or hill;
Ne'er saw I, never felt, a calm so deep!
The river glideth at his own sweet will:
Dear God! the very houses seem asleep;
And all that mighty heart is lying still!

3.8.6 Understanding and responding to texts B

Deep dive into analysis

1 Blake uses repetition in stanza two. How does this help to communicate a lack of hope for the people of London?

____

____

2 Explain how Blake's metaphor 'mind-forg'd manacles' is a powerful comment on how he sees the powerlessness of the working poor.

3 In stanza three Blake criticises the Church, which traditionally would have supported the poor. How does his choice of language do this?

4 Comment on how Blake's final stanza successfully communicates his despair over what London offers its people.

5 In Wordsworth's poem, what impression of London does the poet give through his word choices of 'fair' and 'majesty'?

6 How does the use of the stylistic device of personification in lines four and five help to convey a more sympathetic view of London in comparison with Blake's poem?

7 Personification is used later in the poem to bring together the urban and the natural scene for Wordsworth. Write the lines from the poem that show the poet is inspired by nature and explain how his word choices help to illustrate this.

3.8.7 Expressing ideas and composing texts A

Extended writing: comparative analysis

Your goal: To use the structural conventions of analytical writing purposefully by:

- including a clear thesis statement
- using well-crafted topic sentences that progress your analytical thinking
- using clear quotations to support and explain your ideas
- constructing a rhetorically effective conclusion

Your task:

Both Blake and Wordsworth are talking about the same city, at the same time; yet their voices and perspectives on London are very different. In your English notebook write a comparative response to the following question:

How do Romantic poets share certain stylistic characteristics while maintaining their individual voices?

Try using the sentence starters below to help show your understanding of the poems.

In William Blake's poem 'London' he shows it to be a place of ...

He communicates his perspective through a variety of language choices such as ...

On the other hand, William Wordsworth offers a different view: that London is a city ...

He illustrates his ideas by using language that contrasts with Blake's, such as ...

Words and phrases that can be helpful when you are comparing texts include:

although	**both**	**but**	**however**	**despite**	**in comparison**
in contrast	**likewise**	**yet**	**unlike**	**while**	**on the other hand**

As you compare the perspectives in the poems, see if you can use any of these.

What has been the lasting impact of Romanticism?

The generation immediately following Wordsworth and Blake are known as the Second Generation Romantics. They were at their height of influence in the 1820s. Arguably the most famous of these poets are:

- Lord Byron
- Percy Bysshe Shelley
- John Keats
- John Clare.

Beyond the nineteenth century, numerous modern poets have been influenced by the Romanticism movement, drawing inspiration from its emphasis on individualism, nature, emotion and imagination.

3.8.8 Reading, viewing and listening to texts

In pairs, choose one of the poets listed and find three or four of their most famous poems.

As you read with your partner, highlight any parts of the poem that you think echo the ideals and features of Romantic poetry.

W. B. Yeats (1865–1939)

An Irish poet and Nobel laureate.

Dylan Thomas (1914–1953)

A Welsh poet known for his rich and vivid language.

Sylvia Plath (1932–1963)

An American poet and novelist, known for her confessional style and the exploration of personal emotions.

Seamus Heaney (1939–2013)

An Irish poet who wrote of landscape, history and the mythology of Ireland.

Mary Oliver (1935–2019)

An American poet celebrated for her nature poetry.

3.8.9 Expressing ideas and composing texts A

Paired class presentation

Your goal: To clearly communicate complex ideas and information to your peers by:

- selecting purposeful strategies to position your peers and evoke an emotional response
- using intentional verbal and non-verbal language, including gestures, to emphasise your key points, enhance engagement and clarify meaning

- delivering your ideas and argument with engaging use of intonation, emphasis, volume, pace and timing
- using transitionary language to signal the development of ideas through language choices, structure and presentational features.

Your task:

As a pair, choose ONE poem from your curated collection that you think most effectively conveys the spirit of the Romantic movement.

Using analysis of this poem as a focus, create a class presentation reflecting on how the legacy of Romanticism continues to shape contemporary poetry.

3.8.10 Chapter reflection

1 We live in a time of great environmental change, and in many ways so did the Romantic poets. How would you describe a 'modern Romantic'? Can such a thing exist? What do you think their main concerns would be, and why?

2 You will notice that all the Romantic poets we have explored in the chapter are male. Why do you think this is? Research the few female poets who existed at this time and decide whether they too were poets of Romanticism.

3 Let's return to the central inquiry question: ***Is poetry 'simply the best words in the best order'?*** A famous Romantic poet, Samuel Coleridge, made this statement. Reflecting on what you have learnt, to what extent do you agree with him? Discuss this with a partner, or perhaps your teacher would agree to a class debate.

CHAPTER 9: LOVE POETRY – A MATCH MADE IN HEAVEN?

Chapter overview

In this chapter, you will consider how love poetry has been used to console, inspire and challenge ideals of love across the ages by exploring a range of poetic forms.

You will learn about the conventions of love poetry, the symbols of love and how these have changed or remained the same over time. You are invited to reflect upon the different ways love is experienced.

Success criteria: In this chapter, I will be successful when I can ...

- draw on my knowledge of love and poetry to question, challenge and understand new and familiar texts
- be informed and inspired by reading, viewing and listening to poetry
- analyse how poetic forms, features and language can shape meaning
- understand how meaningful connections can be made between love poems across time
- express my ideas of love in my compositions.

Chapter inquiry questions

- What is love?
- What were the first love poems like?
- What are the codes and conventions of love poetry?
- How do poets represent notions of love?
- Has love poetry endured into the twenty-first century?

Key vocabulary

- Courtly love
- Sonnet
- Free verse

What is love?

Over the centuries poets, artists and philosophers have tried to define love. Why are we attracted to one person and not another? What is the difference between 'being in love' and 'loving'? If love is a universal emotion, how have our expectations of it evolved?

Originally created by Kim Casali as a way of expressing her feelings for her husband, the 'Love is ...' cartoon was one of longest running cartoon strips in history.

3.9.1 Warm-up

Casali's cartoons always began with the phrase 'Love is ...' and featured the same cartoon characters.

Scan the QR code to research the range.

Discuss with a partner what assumptions people might have about love.

Together, reflect on what creates and perpetuates our assumptions.

Some assumptions to get you started might be that:

- love leads to marriage
- love is always about romance
- everyone can find love.

3.9.2 Expressing ideas and composing texts A

1 Imitating Casali's style, design a modern 'Love is ...' cartoon that embodies a representation you think is important for teenagers of the twenty-first century.

When you have finished, share your cartoons as a whole class and discuss with your peers.

2 Write your final thoughts below, completing this sentence starter.

In the twenty-first century, love is ...

Scan the QR code to read this article from The Conversation *titled 'What is Love?'*

What were the first love poems like?

Love poetry seems to have been part of the literary canon since time began. One of the oldest love poems is 'The Love Song of Shu-Sin', discovered by archaeologist Samuel Noah Kramer and believed to have been part of a marriage ritual, the symbolic wedding of a Mesopotamian king to Inanna, a Sumerian goddess of love. The poem would likely have been read by the bride to the groom in the hope that the goddess would bless their union.

Here is an extract from it.

Bridegroom, dear to my heart,
Goodly is your beauty, honeysweet,
Lion, dear to my heart,
Goodly is your beauty, honeysweet.

You have captivated me, let me stand tremblingly before you.
Bridegroom, I would be taken by you to the bedchamber,
You have captivated me, let me stand tremblingly before you.
Lion, I would be taken by you to the bedchamber.

3.9.3 Reading, viewing and listening to texts

1 What images can you identify here that represent love?

2 Do you think this representation of love still resonates with a modern audience? Justify your thinking.

Another of the oldest love poems comes from a book in the Bible called the 'Song of Solomon' or 'Song of Songs'. This also encapsulates emotions of love between newly married lovers. This extract is from chapter 1, verses 15–17:

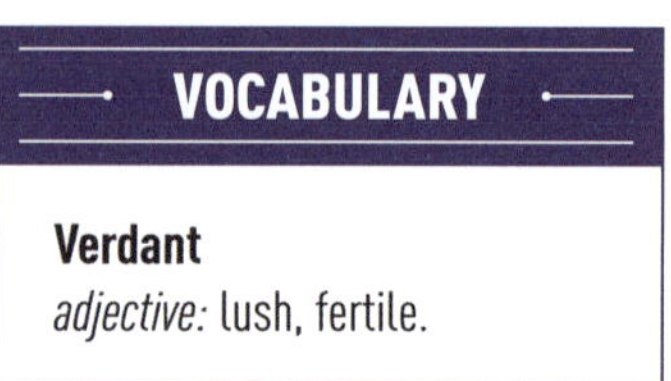

He
15 How beautiful you are, my darling!
Oh, how beautiful!
Your eyes are doves.

She
16 How handsome you are, my beloved!
Oh, how charming!
And our bed is **verdant**.

He
17 The beams of our house are cedars;
our rafters are firs.

3.9.4 Understanding and responding to texts A

1 What literary device has been employed in 'Your eyes are doves' and what does this tell the reader about how the man sees his wife?

2 The wife describes their marriage bed as 'verdant' – what do you think this refers to?

3 **After reading these extracts, what conclusions might you come to in regard to the nature of the earliest love poetry? Justify your thinking using quotations from the poems.**

What are the codes and conventions of love poetry?

In all genres of literature there are accepted **codes** and **conventions** that often govern how meaning is made, communicated and interpreted – and poetry is no different. These codes and conventions can be connected to the structure or form of a poem, or the symbols used to communicate ideas. The codes and conventions associated with love poetry have changed over time.

In medieval love poetry, many of the images presented to the reader were religious, where love was believed to be something divine or not of the earthly world. This was because medieval love poetry embodied the ideal of what is known as **courtly love**.

LANGUAGE

Courtly love = the medieval tradition of love between a knight and a married noblewoman.

The courtly lover existed to serve his lady. Ironically, the lady would be already married and so inaccessible. Marriage at this time was usually the result of a business interest or the seal of a power alliance. Ultimately, the lover saw himself as serving the all-powerful god of Love, worshipping his lady-saint. Faithlessness was considered a sin both against lover and against God and thus courtly love was never consummated, but was purely romantic.

This poetry of perfect, and often unrequited, love was developed through the conventions of the sonnet form, which adhered to a strict structure. The Italian poet Petrarch was famous for his sonnets and his style was named after him. Petrarch wrote over 300 sonnets to a married lady to express his admiration and romantic love for her.

A sonnet has 14 lines divided into an *octave* (a stanza of eight lines) and a *sestet* (a stanza of six lines). The *volta* (or the change) happens in the ninth line.

A traditional Petrarchan sonnet has a rhyme scheme of **ABBAABBACDCDCD** and each line is written in *iambic pentameter*.

3.9.5 Reading, viewing and listening to texts

English poet and playwright William Shakespeare adapted the sonnet form. Read the following example.

Sonnet 116
Let me not to the marriage of true minds
Admit **impediments**. Love is not love
Which alters when it alteration finds,
Or bends with the remover to remove.
O no! it is an **ever-fixed mark**
That looks on **tempests** and is never shaken;
It is the star to every wand'ring **bark**,
Whose worth's unknown, although his height be taken.
Love's not Time's fool, though rosy lips and cheeks
Within his bending **sickle's** compass come;
Love alters not with his brief hours and weeks,
But bears it out even to the edge of doom.
If this be error and upon me prov'd,
I never writ, nor no man ever lov'd.

VOCABULARY

Impediments
noun: obstacles.

Ever-fixed mark
noun: permanent feeling.

Tempests
noun: storms, either of climate or of temper.

Bark
noun: boat.

Sickle
noun: a curved tool used for harvesting wheat which, since the fifteenth century, has been associated with the personification of death as the Grim Reaper.

1 Read the Shakespearean sonnet with a friend, and together annotate it to show your understanding of sonnet features such as structure, rhyme and figurative language.

2 Which features used by Shakespeare are the same as Petrarch's and which are different?

Beyond the conventions of structure, Sonnet 116 includes another code of love poetry – that **love is eternal**, and can transcend even death.

3 Read lines 9–12 again.

- With a partner, discuss how these lines explore the eternal convention of love, even beyond death.
- Write your thoughts below as bullet points.

- ______________________________
- ______________________________
- ______________________________
- ______________________________

Love poetry is usually written by a **single persona to their beloved**, and their **beloved is often idealised** and worshipped, despite or sometimes because of their flaws. Some love poetry explores the confusion or despair of love lost or love unrequited.

Traditionally, love poetry uses **common symbols** such as the seasons of spring or summer, light, hearts, flowers and figurative language connected to nature to emphasise the purity and strength of love.

3.9.6 Reading, viewing and listening to texts

Read and annotate the poem below, identifying as many of the conventions of love poetry as you can.

A Red, Red Rose

by Robert Burns

O my Luve is like a red, red rose
That's newly sprung in June;
O my Luve is like the melody
That's sweetly played in tune.

So fair art thou, my **bonnie lass**,
So deep in luve am I;
And I will luve thee still, my dear,
Till a' the seas **gang dry**.

Till a' the seas gang dry, my dear,
And the rocks melt wi' the sun;
I will love thee still, my dear,
While the sands o' life shall run.

And fare thee **weel**, my only luve!
And fare thee weel awhile!
And I will come again, my luve,
Though it were ten thousand mile.

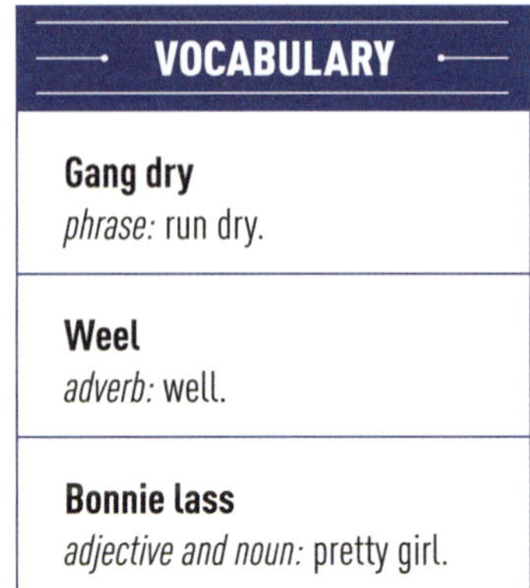
VOCABULARY

Gang dry
phrase: run dry.

Weel
adverb: well.

Bonnie lass
adjective and noun: pretty girl.

How do poets represent notions of love?

As you know now, there are some clear codes and conventions that let a reader know they are reading a love poem. Let's delve a little deeper into the effect of these features, thinking about how they influence our own views on love and how they can be subverted.

3.9.7 Reading, viewing and listening to texts

The American poet E. E. Cummings (1894–1962) was unusual for his time because he rarely used punctuation or capital letters in his poetry. This was part of **free verse**, which didn't use a rigid structure like a sonnet.

Read the following poem.

[i carry your heart with me(i carry it in]

By E. E. Cummings

i carry your heart with me(i carry it in
my heart)i am never without it(anywhere
i go you go,my dear;and whatever is done
by only me is your doing,my darling)
                                                      i fear
no fate(for you are my fate,my sweet)i want
no world(for beautiful you are my world,my true)
and it's you are whatever a moon has always meant

and whatever a sun will always sing is you

here is the deepest secret nobody knows
(here is the root of the root and the bud of the bud
and the sky of the sky of a tree called life;which grows
higher than soul can hope or mind can hide)
and this is the wonder that's keeping the stars apart

i carry your heart(i carry it in my heart)

3.9.8 Understanding and responding to texts A

1 Why do you think E. E. Cummings has used brackets (or parentheses) in this poem?

2 One of the common motifs in love poetry is the heart. How has E. E. Cummings used this effectively as a metaphor for love?

3 In the following lines, Cummings uses images of nature, which is another common motif.

(here is the root of the root and the bud of the bud
and the sky of the sky of a tree called life;which grows
higher than soul can hope or mind can hide)

Comment on how these enhance the central purpose of his poem – to communicate his feelings to his beloved.

Let's look at another poem. *After Love*, by Sara Teasdale, is about love lost and how, without love, the world seems drab. The persona conveys sorrow and bitterness.

After Love

by Sara Teasdale

There is no magic any more,
We meet as other people do,
You work no miracle for me
Nor I for you.

You were the wind and I the sea—
There is no splendor any more,
I have grown listless as the pool
Beside the shore.

But though the pool is safe from storm
And from the tide has found surcease,
It grows more bitter than the sea,
For all its peace.

4 Comment on how Teasdale uses water as a symbol to convey her feelings about her lost love.

Make sure that you refer to the poem using quotations and literary terminology.

3.9.9 Expressing ideas and composing texts A and B

When we lose something or someone we value, we often feel, as Teasdale describes in her poem, that 'There is no magic anymore'. Without a close friend or partner, life can seem very grey whereas with them it was filled with colour.

The Australian poet Lisa Brockwell wrote 'The Ballad of Monday Morning' about her experience of loss as she left her husband at the airport to work away from home, while she went home to look after the home and family. You can find her poem here:

Scan the QR code to access 'The Ballad of Monday Morning' by Lisa Brockwell.

Use this idea of love lost as inspiration for a piece of original writing. In your English notebook, write a poem or a short narrative.

Has love poetry endured into the twenty-first century?

You have learnt in this chapter that love is a universal and timeless theme that poets have been writing about since before the fifth century BCE. But is love poetry still relevant, and if so, how has it evolved for a modern audience?

3.9.10 Reading, viewing and listening to texts

Verse voyage: navigating the seas of twenty-first century love poetry

One of the ways that poetry has remained relevant is by embracing different modes, such as **performance** or **spoken word** poetry. Working in a small group, access the links via the QR codes below to experience love poetry with all the vibrancy and poignancy of our modern age.

'To the girl who works at Starbucks' by Rudy Francisco

'For women who are difficult to love' by Warsan Shire

'When love arrives' by Sarah Kay and Phil Kaye

Each group member should watch and listen to at least TWO of the poems listed.

Write your thoughts and feelings after each performance – use these questions as prompts:

- What is the message?
- What was interesting or original about the way the theme of love was represented?
- What words or phrases stood out to you and why?
- Was this engaging? Justify your answer.

Share your ideas with your group and reflect on the discussion by completing the thinking routine below.

Connect	Extend	Challenge
What discussion ideas connected to your own thinking?	What discussion ideas extended your own thinking?	What discussion ideas challenged your own thinking?

3.9.11 Expressing ideas and composing texts A and B 

After listening to these examples of love poetry, how would you respond to the inquiry question, ***Has love poetry endured into the twenty-first century?***

Analyse and evaluate the enduring theme of love in poetry. You can do this by:

- reflecting on the ideas that underpin love in the twenty-first century
- identifying a range of stylistic features, codes and conventions that shape meaning
- commenting upon how these features might be engaging to a modern audience.

Write a detailed response in your English notebook addressing the question and success criteria above.

3.9.12 Chapter reflection 

In this chapter, you have learnt about the enduring theme of love in poetry from the earliest of times to the modern day.

1 As you reflect on the poems you have read, viewed and listened to, consider this: Does literature give us idealistic expectations of love?

Discuss this with a friend. What did you decide?

2 Which poem from this chapter really embodies the quotation in our unit inquiry question, that ***poetry is 'simply the best words in the best order'***? Try to justify your response by picking out a line you found most effective and explain why.

3 Revisit the very first activity you completed in this unit – you drew a 'Love is ...' cartoon in the spirit of Kim Casali. Has your view about love changed from studying the poems in this chapter? If so, how? If not, why not?

4 If your view of love has changed, you might like to design a new cartoon here.

Unit 3: **Summative assessment**

The summative assessment options below provide opportunities to demonstrate your achievement of the following outcomes and focus areas.

Outcome and focus area	EN5-RVL-01 Reading, viewing and listening to texts	EN5-URA-01 Understanding and responding to texts A	EN5-URB-01 Understanding and responding to texts B	EN5-ECA-01 Expressing ideas and composing texts A
Content point	Reading, viewing and listening for meaning	Code and convention	Perspective and context	Writing
		Connotation, imagery and symbol		Speaking
	Reflecting		Argument and authority	Text features
			Style	

Option 1: Deep diving into discursive writing

Choose one of the poets whose work you have encountered and enjoyed in the course of this unit. They can be living or not.

You are a journalist and have been commissioned to interview the poet for the *New Yorker* magazine.

PART 1

Design the questions you would ask them and the responses they would give.

PART 2

Write a discursive article, using your knowledge of their poetry and context, as well as what you have crafted in Part 1. Your article is responding to this prompt: The contemporary appeal of [insert renowned poet] and their enduring impact on literature and society.

Be guided by the following questions when planning and writing.

- How have their experiences shaped the voice of your chosen poet?
- What are the central concerns of their poetry and how are these communicated in an engaging way for a contemporary audience?
- What is or has been their influence on the literary landscape?
- Has their commentary on social, cultural or political issues been a force in their poetry? If so, how?
- What have other literary critics said about them and their work?

PART 3

Peer reflection

Read an article written by a peer and respond on whether or not you would be inclined to read any of the work of their chosen poet. When you make your judgement, consider:

- how engagingly and persuasively they have argued their case
- how well-chosen their examples are
- how accessible the poetry is for you.

Option 2: Poetry aloud!

Poetry is often said to be better experienced when read aloud so that the cadence of the rhyme and rhythm can be fully appreciated. In this unit you have experienced some spoken word or performance poetry.

Craft your own work for this style of poetry and perform it to your peers – either in a 'live' performance or by making a video. (Your teacher might even put them all together to create a Poetry Slam!)

Be guided by the following to plan and write your piece.

- Choose a topic that resonates with you so your delivery is passionate and engaging for your audience.
- Adapt your language for your audience – for example, a school audience will mean you cannot use inappropriate or offensive language.
- Grab your audience from the outset – beginnings are important!
- Experiment, experiment, experiment – with language, with rhyme and with rhythm – to ensure you get a steady flow, which will result in a dynamic performance.
- Include lots of phonological devices such as onomatopoeia, alliteration and assonance to help the rhythm.

And in performance:

- Practise performing to anyone who is willing!
- Make eye contact with different audience members.
- Practise using non-verbal communication strategies such as pausing, gesticulation and facial expression to complement the words of your poem.

Option 3: Analytical essay

Poetry stems from our experiences and emotions and this distilled form helps us to choose the best words and organise them in the best way. Sometimes poets write about love, or nature, or change, or even the craft of writing poetry itself. Draw on all your knowledge of poets and poetry from the unit and from your own reading to respond to the following question:

How do poets respond to or challenge prevailing notions of love within their respective contexts?

To write a good analytical essay, remember to:

- develop and sustain a clear thesis and argument
- start each paragraph with a topic sentence that links to the question
- use evidence and quotations accurately and appropriately
- identify a wide range of poetic terminology and comment on how it creates and shapes meaning
- include a thoughtful conclusion in response to the question and complete your argument convincingly.

Assessment as learning: self-assessment

Does my composition:

- ☐ use clear and adventurous vocabulary which is appropriate to the task?
- ☐ reflect a good knowledge and understanding of poetic terminology?
- ☐ reveal an authentic engagement with the poetic genre?

How effectively did my plan and drafts help me to draft and revise my composition?

____

____

____

What are two strengths of my response?

____

____

What area/s of my response do I need to refine further?

____

____

UNIT 04

Unlocking Shakespeare's craft

Unit inquiry question:
Does Shakespeare speak to us today?

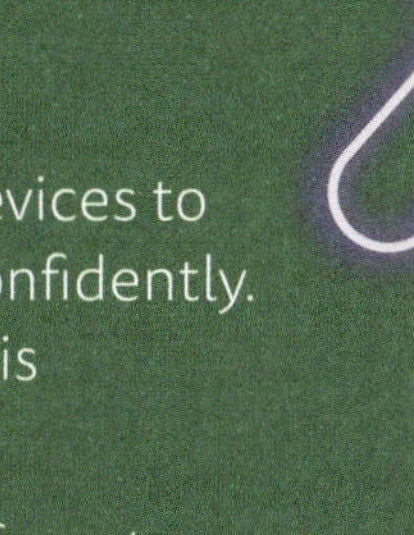

Students will learn about Shakespeare's language and dramatic devices to equip them to read, view and understand Shakespeare's works confidently. This will enable them to appreciate and interpret the artistry of his characters and storytelling.

This unit has been broken into three chapters, which each look at a different aspect of texts and the world and raise additional inquiry questions.

Chapter 10

The poet's pen creates the shapes

An opportunity for students to learn about Shakespeare's language and form, and how they are used to create complex and dynamic characters.

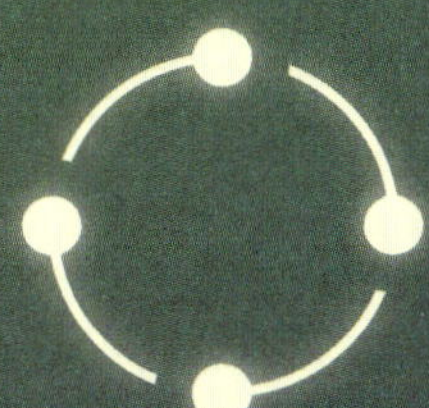

Chapter 11

Shattered ambitions – *Macbeth*

An exploration of the characters Macbeth and Lady Macbeth, and their ill-fated relationship.

Chapter 12

'If I be waspish, best beware my sting' – *The Taming of the Shrew*

An examination of The *Taming of the Shrew* and the ways in which societal expectations of men and women often dictated the landscape of their relationships.

The learning activities within each chapter and the summative assessment options (on pages 169–171) provide opportunities to assess student achievement of the following outcomes.

Outcome and focus area	Content point
EN5-RVL-01 **Reading, viewing and listening to texts**	**Reflecting**
	Use reading strategies, and evaluate their effectiveness, when reflecting on the successes and challenges of extended reading
EN5-URA-01 **Understanding and responding to texts A**	**Characterisation**
	Analyse how engaging, dynamic and complex characters are constructed in texts using language features and structures, and use these features and structures in own texts
EN5-URB-01 **Understanding and responding to texts B**	**Theme**
	Appreciate the role of the audience in perceiving themes and how these themes can offer insights into an author's perspective
	Perspective and context
	Understand how the personal perspectives of audiences are a product of historical and cultural contexts
	Appreciate the significance and value of expressions of cultural context in texts constructed using elements of languages and dialects, including Standard Australian English, Aboriginal and/or Torres Strait Islander Languages, and Aboriginal English
	Argument and authority
	Research, select and sequence appropriate evidence from texts and reliable sources to construct cohesive and authoritative arguments
	Evaluate how the authority of a text is continually negotiated and reassessed by readers
	Style
	Evaluate how particular styles in text can be privileged according to context
	Examine the way an author's distinct personal style shapes meaning in their work

EN5-ECA-01 **Expressing ideas and composing texts A**	**Speaking**
	Select effective rhetorical strategies to position an audience and evoke an emotional response
	Communicate complex information, ideas and viewpoints using purposeful verbal and/or nonverbal language, including gestures, to emphasise key points, enhance engagement and clarify meaning
	Deliver spoken, signed or communicated texts with engaging use of intonation, emphasis, volume, pace and timing
	Signal the development of ideas through language, structure and presentational features
	Text features
	Introduce and define complex key ideas, academic concepts and positions for arguments in sustained analytical and persuasive texts
	Use the structural conventions of persuasive texts to purposefully justify opinions and develop expanding arguments, including a focused opening and thesis, logically sequenced elaboration paragraphs, and a conclusion that synthesises complex ideas
	Word-level language
	Use the structural conventions of persuasive texts to purposefully justify opinions and develop expanding arguments, including a focused opening and thesis, logically sequenced elaboration paragraphs, and a conclusion that synthesises complex ideas
EN5-ECB-01 **Expressing ideas and composing texts B**	**Planning, monitoring and revising**
	Develop an effective thesis for extended analytical and persuasive texts that is based on critical thinking about a text or topic
	Plan a progressive sequence of arguments or ideas, and set goals at conceptual, whole text and paragraph levels

CHAPTER 10: THE POET'S PEN CREATES THE SHAPES

Chapter overview

In this chapter, you will learn about Shakespeare's style, and how he crafted complex and dynamic characters. You will explore various aspects of Shakespeare's craft, his language and the forms that define his masterpieces.

Whether you're already familiar with his works or a newcomer to Shakespearean studies, this chapter will help you to appreciate the linguistic craft and theatrical innovation that have made Shakespeare an enduring icon.

Success criteria: In this chapter, I will be successful when I can ...

- analyse how characters are constructed by Shakespeare through language features and structure
- examine the way Shakespeare's distinct personal style shapes meaning in his works
- speak Shakespeare's lines with engaging intonation, emphasis, volume, pace and timing.

Chapter inquiry questions

- What is Shakespearean language?
- How does Shakespeare create characterisation through form?
- How do Shakespeare's soliloquies and monologues contribute to the depth and relatability of his characters?

Key vocabulary

- Blank verse
- Prose
- Iambic pentameter
- Soliloquies
- Monologues

What is Shakespearean language?

As much as it pains many English teachers to admit, many people find Shakespeare challenging to read and understand. There are frequent complaints that he 'doesn't speak English' or that his language is all 'Old English', and disbelief that ordinary people ever spoke like that.

Contrary to what some may believe, Shakespeare did not write in Old English. He wrote in the Early Modern English period, which spanned approximately 1500–1750 and was not quite 100 years old when Shakespeare was writing.

Dictionaries were not published until 1604. English language use at this time was very fluid and malleable and was ever evolving, much like today!

4.10.1 Warm-up

Read the famous sayings based on Shakepearean quotations below.

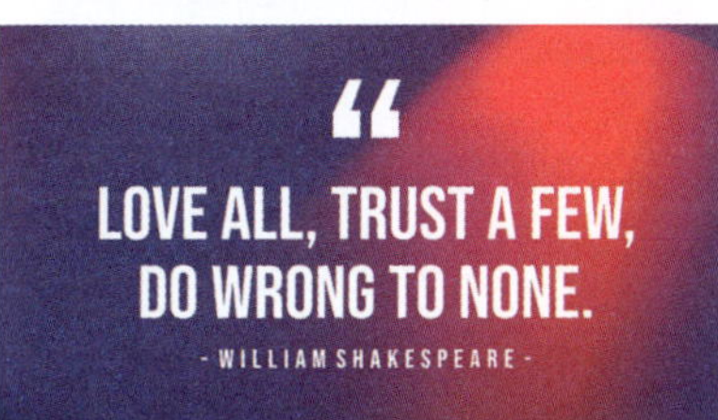

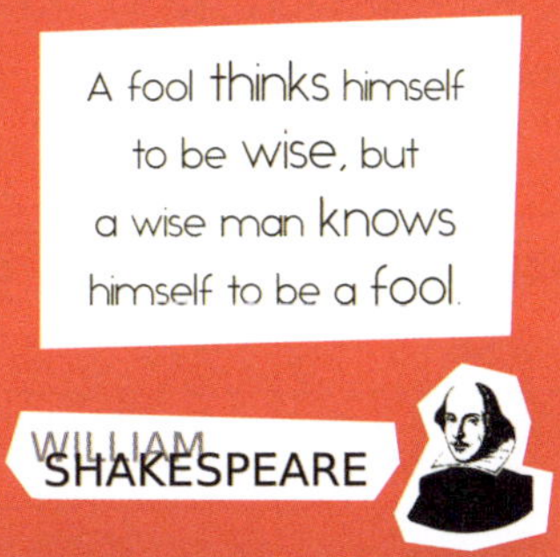

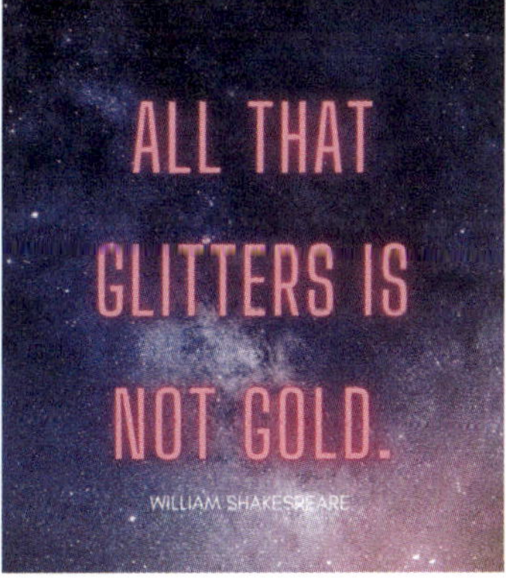

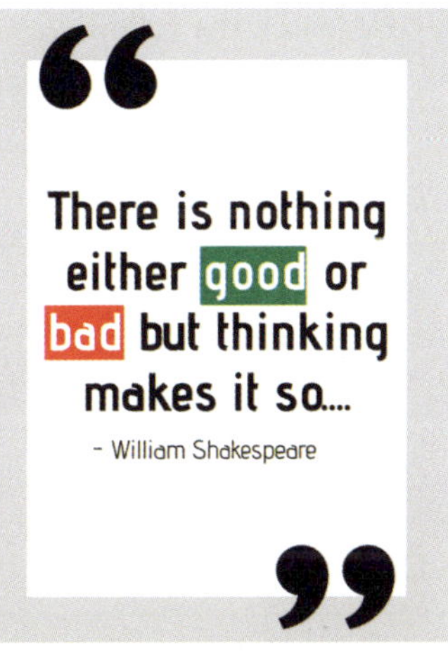

1 Choose the one that you like best. Explain what you think it means.

____

____

2 Re-write it in your own words.

____

____

Shakespeare was writing at a time when writing the English language down was still relatively new. Many of the conventions we are bound by today were yet to be established – it was an exciting time to be a playwright.

Shakespeare invented many words (over 1,700) that we still use today. Not only did he create new words, but he often messed about with existing words. He combined words (e.g. bedroom and eyeball), changed nouns into verbs (e.g. kissing), and added prefixes or suffixes (e.g. worthless). For example, from 'gloom' he invented the word 'gloomy' (in *Titus Andronicus*).

There are some words that haven't stuck, but these only account for five per cent of the words found in Shakespeare's texts.

4.10.2 Reading, viewing and listening to texts

1 Research the following words, invented and used by Shakespeare, and write down the modern meaning. Some have been done for you.

Abhor	Loathe	Mark	
Anon		Nay	No
Art		Retire	
Chuck		Sayeth	
Dost/Doth		Soft	
Draw		Thou/Thy	
Giveth		Want	
Hast	Have	Whence	
Hie		Wherefore	
Maid		Yonder	

Thou versus you

Did you know that English used to have two 'you' forms? It might surprise you to learn that:

'You' = a formal and polite form; also addresses more than one person.

'Thou/thee' = a familiar, intimate form; refers to one person.

2 Read the following speech.

Is this a dagger which I see before me,
The handle toward my hand? Come, let me clutch thee.
I have thee not, and yet I see thee still.
Art thou not, fatal vision, sensible
To feeling as to sight? or art thou but
A dagger of the mind, a false creation,
Proceeding from the heat-oppressed brain?
I see thee yet, in form as palpable
As this which now I draw.

(from *Macbeth*)

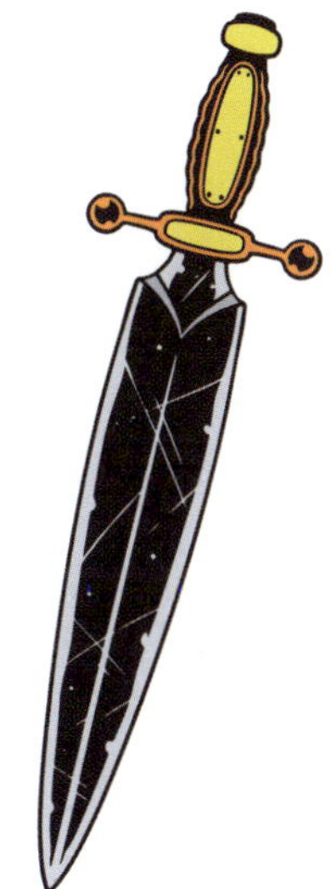

3 Above each underlined word, write the modern-day equivalent.

4 Knowing that 'thee' suggests something slightly different to 'you', explain why Macbeth uses thee when speaking to the dagger.

___

___

___

4.10.3 Expressing ideas and composing texts A

With a partner, write a short dialogue in your English notebook, using words from the vocabulary list and the speech, as well as Shakespearean grammar. Then read your dialogue aloud to the class.

How does Shakespeare create characterisation through form?

Shakespeare's plays are mainly written in three forms: **blank verse**, **rhymed verse** and **prose**. What's really impressive about Shakespeare is the way that he uses the form, structure and rhythm of his writing to communicate something about his characters. We can understand something about them from the way that they speak.

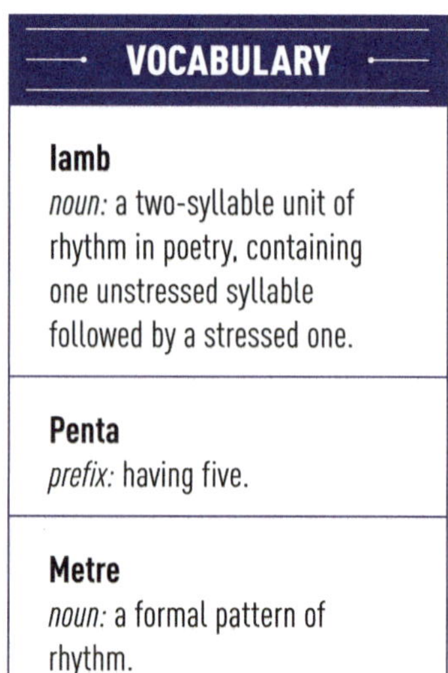

VOCABULARY

Iamb
noun: a two-syllable unit of rhythm in poetry, containing one unstressed syllable followed by a stressed one.

Penta
prefix: having five.

Metre
noun: a formal pattern of rhythm.

Blank verse

Shakespeare, keen to show that the English language was just as 'literary' as Latin, wrote his plays mainly in blank verse, which is like poetry. This enabled him to show how good the English language could be. Blank verse does not rhyme, but it does follow a regular rhythm: a five-beat rhythm, which is known as **iambic pentameter**.

4.10.4 Reading, viewing and listening to texts

With iambic pentameter each line has five beats with an unstressed syllable (-) followed by a stressed syllable (/). The rhythm imitates a heartbeat and is like normal speech stresses.

For example:

- / - / - / - / - /

But soft! What light through yonder window breaks?

- / - / - / - / - /

So fair and foul a day I have not seen

1 In pairs, read aloud these lines clapping out the rhythm.

2 Underline the stressed syllables in these examples.

RICHARD
Now is the winter of our discontent
Made glorious summer by this son of York,
And all the clouds that loured upon our house
In the deep bosom of the ocean buried.

(from *Richard III*)

PETRUCHIO
Say that she rail, why then I'll tell her plain
She sings as sweetly as a nightingale:
Say that she frown, I'll say she looks as clear
As morning roses newly washed with dew ...

(from *The Taming of the Shrew*)

The last word at the end of iambic pentameter is often the most important:

- 'Friends, countrymen, lend me your *ears*.'
- 'To be or not to be, that is the *question*.'
- 'Two loves I have of comfort and *despair*.'

3 Circle the last word in each of the above excerpts from *Richard III* and *The Taming of the Shrew*. Explain how the rhythm emphasises the last word.

A change in the metre is always important to note as it's a clue to a change in the character's thoughts and feelings.

MACBETH
Throw physic to the dogs; I'll none of it.
Come, put mine armour on; give me my staff.
Seyton, send out. Doctor, the thanes fly from me.
Come, sir, dispatch.

(from *Macbeth*)

4 Underline the metre. See if you can identify where the metre changes.

Along with metre, Shakespeare used punctuation to help the actors make meaning of their lines, and to know when to pause and for how long. Commas are short pauses, whereas full-stops, semi-colons, question marks and exclamation marks are long pauses, where the actor would take a breath. These long pauses, when they fall in the middle of a line, are called a **caesura**.

PETRUCHIO
Why, there's a wench! Come on, and kiss me, Kate.

(from *The Taming of the Shrew*)

5 Read aloud both excerpts from *The Taming of the Shrew*, following the punctuation. Discuss with a partner how following the punctuation helped you to trace the character's thoughts.

4.10.5 Understanding and responding to texts A

An **end-stopped** line is when the punctuation is at the end of the verse line. **Enjambment** is when a line runs past the line break and stops at the next punctuation mark. Annotate the enjambment in the previous extracts.

1 Explain the purpose and effect of enjambment.

2 Compare the punctuation and metre in these lines:

PRINCE
For this time all the rest depart away.
You, Capulet, shall go along with me,
And, Montague, come you this afternoon
To know our farther pleasure in this case,
To old Free-town, our common judgment-place.
Once more, on pain of death, all men depart.

(from *Romeo and Juliet*)

CALIBAN
Sometimes a thousand twangling instruments
Will hum about mine ears, and sometime voices,
That, if I then had waked after long sleep,
Will make me sleep again; and then, in dreaming,
The clouds methought would open and show riches
Ready to drop upon me, that when I waked
I cried to dream again.

(from *The Tempest*)

3 The excerpt from *Romeo and Juliet* was written much earlier than the one from *The Tempest* (one of his last plays). Explain what this might tell us about Shakespeare.

Half lines or pick-up lines

At times, a character is given an incomplete line. This is called a **half line** (even if it is less or more than half the five beats). You can see this in Caliban last line above.

4.10.6 Understanding and responding to texts A

Why is the line incomplete? Was the character interrupted? Or could they be pausing? Hesitating or waiting?

Often, Shakespeare creates half lines to be **shared** lines. Two or more characters share their lines, with the iambic pentameter divided between them.

Let's read an example from *Macbeth*.

- / - /

LADY MACBETH: Did not you speak?

-

MACBETH: When?

/

LADY MACBETH: Now?

- / - /

As I descended?

What is the effect of the shared lines?

______

______

______

Rhymed verse

As well as blank verse, Shakespeare also uses rhyme. Often, a **rhymed** couplet sums up a character's speech, ends a scene and sometimes sets up the next scene. Here's an example:

VIOLA
O Time, thou must untangle this, not I.
It is too hard a knot for me t'untie.

(from *Twelfth Night*)

4.10.7 Understanding and responding to texts A

Rhyme is often used to indicate special characters: for example, the witches in *Macbeth*.

Double, double, toil and trouble
Fire burn and cauldron bubble

Notice how the rhythm (not iambic) and rhyme give the witches' lines a distinct sound. Explain what it sounds like and why.

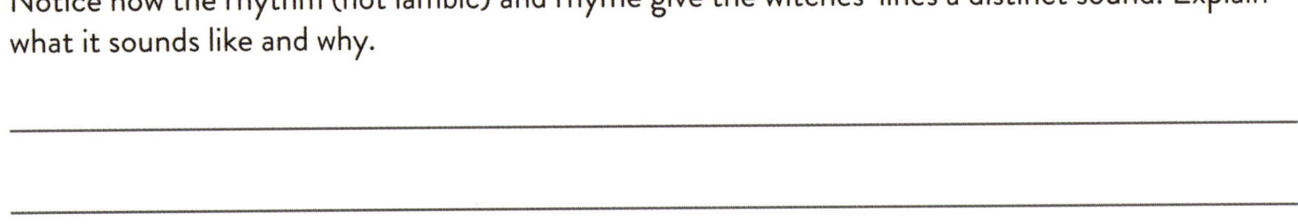

Prose

During Shakespeare's time, plays were written in blank verse. Shakespeare's use of **prose** is another example of his inventiveness and willingness to go against convention. Prose is everyday language, so there's no rhythm or metre in the lines. It is mainly used for common characters (e.g. murderers, servants and porters), for comic and domestic scenes, and to indicate familiarity, secrecy or conspiracy.

Here's an example from the Porter in *Macbeth*:

> **PORTER**
> **Faith, sir, we were carousing till the second cock, and drink, sir, is a great provoker of three things.**

However, there are times when important characters speak in prose. Prose makes the character sound natural and creates a conversational tone.

> **IAGO**
> **It is merely a lust of the blood and a permission of the will. Come, be a man! Drown thyself? Drown cats and blind puppies.**

4.10.8 Understanding and responding to texts A

When a character who usually speaks in verse suddenly shifts to prose, it can show a change in their emotions or thoughts.

Let's read an example from Macbeth.

> **LADY MACBETH**
> **Here's the smell of the blood still; all the perfumes of Arabia will not sweeten this little hand. O, O, O.**

1 Lady Macbeth is sleepwalking and is experiencing great turmoil and anguish. Shakespeare writes her lines in prose instead of blank verse to indicate a change in the character, in lieu of stage directions. What's the purpose and effect?

Here's an example from *Hamlet*.

> HAMLET
> I have of late – but wherefore I know not – lost all my mirth, forgone all custom of exercise; and indeed it goes so heavily with my disposition that this goodly frame, the earth, seems to me a sterile promontory. This most excellent canopy, the air, look you, this brave o'erhanging firmament, this majestical roof fretted with golden fire – why, it appears no other thing to me than a foul and pestilent congregation of vapours.

2 Even though Hamlet is a prince, Shakespeare interrupts his verse and writes in prose. Why do you think he does this? What's the effect?

3 Why does it matter? If you observe the changes, you gain insight into Shakespeare's intentions. Explain how the form of Shakespeare's writing tells us something about his characters.

How do Shakespeare's soliloquies and monologues contribute to the depth and relatability of his characters?

Shakespeare's speeches are powerful tools for exploring characters' motivations, thoughts and feelings. These introspective speeches provide insight into the psychological depth of his characters. In Shakespeare's plays there are two main forms: **soliloquies** and **monologues**.

VOCABULARY

Soliloquy
noun: when a character speaks their thoughts aloud to the audience. It's just the character and the audience.

Monologue
noun: an uninterrupted speech that characters make to other characters on stage.

4.10.9 Reading, viewing and listening to texts

Read Mark Antony's speech from *Julius Caesar* beginning with 'Friends, Romans, countrymen, lend me your ears' and ending with 'And I must pause till it come back to me'.

1 Explain how the rhythm and punctuation creates pace and pausing.

____

____

____

2 How do Shakespeare's stylistic devices make this speech inspirational/engaging? Select a device and explain its effect.

____

____

____

3 Find two different performances of this speech. Compare these – outline the similarities and differences between the two. Which did you prefer and why?

____

____

____

Soliloquies allow the character to share their thoughts, feelings and motivations directly with the audience. Shakespeare uses soliloquies for the character to reveal their deeper thoughts to the audience.

4.10.10 Reading, viewing and listening to texts

One of the most famous lines from Shakespeare, 'To be or not to be', comes from a speech from the play *Hamlet*. This speech has been performed, interpreted and reinterpreted time and time again, and will continue to be so.

Read Hamlet's speech.

DISCUSS

Discuss the following: Who is speaking? Who is listening? What's the message? What is the character wanting or not wanting in this speech?

IDENTIFY

Highlight examples of end-stopped lines, enjambment and caesura.

INTERPRET

Illustrate two or three key images that capture Hamlet's inner thoughts. Draw these around the soliloquy.

To be, or not to be, that is the question:
Whether 'tis nobler in the mind to suffer
The slings and arrows of outrageous fortune,
Or to take arms against a sea of troubles
And by opposing end them. To die – to sleep,
No more; and by a sleep to say we end
The heart-ache and the thousand natural shocks
That flesh is heir to: 'tis a consummation
Devoutly to be wish'd. To die, to sleep;
To sleep, perchance to dream – ay, there's the rub:
For in that sleep of death what dreams may come,
When we have shuffled off this mortal coil,
Must give us pause – there's the respect
That makes calamity of so long life.
For who would bear the whips and scorns of time,
Th'oppressor's wrong, the proud man's contumely,
The pangs of dispriz'd love, the law's delay,
The insolence of office, and the spurns
That patient merit of th'unworthy takes,
When he himself might his quietus make
With a bare bodkin? Who would fardels bear,
To grunt and sweat under a weary life,
But that the dread of something after death,
The undiscover'd country, from whose bourn
No traveller returns, puzzles the will,
And makes us rather bear those ills we have
Than fly to others that we know not of?
Thus conscience does make cowards of us all,
And thus the native hue of resolution
Is sicklied o'er with the pale cast of thought,
And enterprises of great pitch and moment
With this regard their currents turn awry
And lose the name of action.

IDENTIFY

Is it written in blank verse or prose? Mark out the rhythm. Circle the words that are emphasised. Does it change at all?

IDENTIFY

Highlight some stylistic devices (e.g. figurative language, direct address, repetition, rhetorical question, etc.).

4.10.11 Expressing ideas and composing texts A

1 In groups, find another Shakespearean soliloquy. Analyse the soliloquy and present your findings to the class.

2 Choose one of the previous speeches and write a modern-day version. Re-write it using modern language and references, but maintain the essential meaning, emotions and key ideas.

4.10.12 Chapter reflection

1 What are some of the common misconceptions or attitudes towards Shakespeare?

2 What was one thing that you have learnt about Shakespeare and his writing that has helped you to have confidence with reading, understanding and appreciating his plays?

3 Outline one activity from the chapter that helped with your learning.

4 Is there anything that you still don't understand?

5 Let's return to the unit inquiry question: ***Does Shakespeare speak to us today?*** This chapter has encouraged you to explore Shakespeare's language and form. Outline how reading a variety of excerpts from his plays has given you an appreciation of the ways that Shakespeare can still speak to us. Discuss as a group.

CHAPTER 11: SHATTERED AMBITIONS – *MACBETH*

Chapter overview

In this chapter, you will explore whether Shakespeare still has anything meaningful to say to a modern audience through his play *Macbeth*.

It has been said that Shakespeare's characters reflect our own selves back to us. You will examine the ways in which Shakespeare speaks to us through his characterisation of Macbeth and Lady Macbeth, how he demonstrates the downfall of their relationship, and how that psychologically and emotionally impacts them.

In your responses and compositions, you will be invited to construct creative responses to demonstrate your interpretation of Shakespeare's characters.

Success criteria: In this chapter, I will be successful when I can ...

- analyse how engaging, dynamic and complex characters are constructed in texts using language features and structures, and how to use these
- evaluate how the authority of Macbeth is continually negotiated and reassessed by interpreting characters and creating compositions
- examine the way Shakespeare's distinct personal style shapes meaning.

Chapter inquiry questions

- Who are the Macbeths?
- What dramatic devices are used to construct characters?

Key vocabulary

- Soliloquy
- Characterisation

Who are the Macbeths?

The Macbeths, one of the most famous of Shakespeare's power couples, are a team. Everyone (or at least nearly everyone) knows they adore each other; they are the dream couple.

Macbeth is the Thane of Glamis and married to Lady Macbeth. He is a brave and successful captain in King Duncan's army.

Macbeth and Lady Macbeth are intricately linked, each essential to the other's ascent towards their ultimate goals within the play. According to The Kennedy Centre, *Macbeth* is the tragedy of political ambition. A brave Scottish general named Macbeth receives a prophecy from a trio of witches that one day he will become King of Scotland. Spurred to action by his wife, Macbeth murders the King, Duncan, and soon becomes a tyrannical ruler.

This chapter will help you to see that the play is really about the couple and their relationship, and whether it can withstand the tragedy and turmoil that comes their way. We learn about the characters through the heights and depths of their relationship.

4.11.1 Warm-up

Compose an opening, here, or in your English notebook, to a narrative using this image as your prompt. Make your descriptions focus on creating **character**.

Include an active beginning, varying sentence lengths, a simile or metaphor, and adventurous adjectives/verbs.

4.11.2 Reading, viewing and listening to texts

In Act 1, Scene 2, we hear about the hero before we meet him. Both the captain and Ross report to King Duncan the progress of the battle. Read their descriptions of the battle and Macbeth.

IDENTIFY

Underline what is said about Macbeth.

VOCABULARY

Valour/valor
noun: great courage in the face of danger.

INTERPRET

The captain refers to Macbeth as being Valor's minion. He personifies Valor and suggests that Macbeths is Valor's servant. Interpret what you think the captain is suggesting about Macbeth.

CAPTAIN
Doubtful it stood,
As two spent swimmers that do cling together
And choke their art. The merciless Macdonwald –
Worthy to be a rebel, for to that
The multiplying villainies of nature
Do swarm upon him – from the Western Isles
Of kerns and gallowglasses is supplied,
And fortune, on his damnèd quarrel smiling,
Showed like a rebel's whore. But all's too weak,
For brave Macbeth – well he deserves that name –
Disdaining fortune, with his brandished steel,
Which smoked with bloody execution,
Like Valor's minion carved out his passage
Till he faced the slave;
Which ne'er shook hands, nor bade farewell to him,
Till he unseamed him from the nave to th' chops,
And fixed his head upon our battlements.

DISCUSS

Discuss the imagery used to describe Macbeth in battle. What does it suggest about Macbeth as a soldier?

VOCABULARY

Nave
noun: belly button.

Chops
noun: jaw.

1 What are your first impressions of Macbeth?

____

____

____

2 Read the rest of the scene and identify what other things characters (for example, Ross and King Duncan) say about Macbeth. Pay attention to the verbs associated with Macbeth and what they suggest.

____

____

____

4.11.3 Understanding and responding to texts A

The captain's and Ross' language is full of heroic terms and imagery. What traits does Shakespeare emphasise in *Macbeth*?

Act 1, Scene 5: 'My dearest partner of greatness'

In Act 1, Scene 5 we meet Lady Macbeth for the first time as she is reading a letter from her husband. Imagine how many times she has read it, studied it, even memorised parts. This is an important scene as it shows us something about the characters and their relationship.

4.11.4 Reading, viewing and listening to texts

Lady Macbeth: 'Fill me ... top-full of direst cruelty'

1 Read the first thirty lines where Lady Macbeth reads Macbeth's letter. Outline what we learn about Lady Macbeth and Macbeth.

Lady Macbeth	Macbeth

2 Which word do you think best describes Lady Macbeth's reaction to receiving her husband's letter – disappointed, pleased, excited, bored, determined, interested, uncontrolled? Support your view with a quotation from the text.

3 Discuss what you think this tells us about their relationship.

4.11.5 Understanding and responding to texts A

Read Lady Macbeth's speech:

INTERPRET

Symbolism Ravens are ill-omens and were seen as heralds of misfortune or death. Discuss why the raven's cry is 'hoarse'.

Mortal thoughts are deadly thoughts (i.e. thoughts of murder).

VOCABULARY

Gall
noun: bitterness

The **raven** himself is hoarse
That croaks the fatal entrance of Duncan
Under my battlements. Come, you spirits
That tend on **mortal thoughts**, unsex me here,
And fill me from the crown to the toe top-full
Of direst cruelty! Make thick my blood;
Stop up the access and passage to remorse,
That no compunctious visitings of nature
Shake my fell purpose, nor keep peace between
The effect and it! Come to my woman's breasts,
And take my milk for **gall**, you murdering ministers,
Wherever in your sightless substances
You wait on nature's mischief! Come, thick night,
And pall thee in the dunnest smoke of hell,
That my keen knife see not the wound it makes,
Nor heaven peep through the blanket of the dark,
To cry 'Hold, hold!'

IDENTIFY

Underline the words that create battle imagery. What does that suggest about Lady Macbeth?

DISCUSS

Discuss with a partner why you think Duncan's entrance to their castle will be 'fatal'?

IDENTIFY

Circle the word 'come'. Think about what the **repetition** is communicating to us about Lady Macbeth's traits.

Lady Macbeth is decisive and strategic. She knows Macbeth lacks ambition and ruthlessness.

1 What conclusions has she drawn and what is Lady Macbeth prepared to do for her husband?

____

____

____

2 Read the conversation between Lady Macbeth and Macbeth. The way that Shakespeare crafts his dialogue gives us lots of information.

DISCUSS

Half-lines: Shakespeare crafts these lines to be shared.

Discuss what that suggests about Lady Macbeth.

MACBETH
My dearest love,
Duncan comes here tonight.

LADY MACBETH
And when goes hence?

MACBETH
Tomorrow, as he purposes.

LADY MACBETH
O, never
Shall sun that morrow see!
Your face, my thane, is as a book where men
May read strange matters. To beguile the time,
Look like the time. Bear welcome in your eye,
Your hand, your tongue. Look like th' innocent flower,
But be the serpent under 't. He that's coming
Must be provided for; and you shall put
This night's great business into my dispatch,
Which shall to all our nights and days to come
Give solely sovereign sway and masterdom.

INTERPRET

The highlighted line is another **half line.** Lady Macbeth pauses, waiting for a reaction. Interpret what reaction Lady Macbeth is waiting for in that pause.

Interpret what reaction Lady Macbeth is waiting for in that pause.

DISCUSS

They are speaking in code. Discuss what Lady Macbeth means when she says, 'provided'.

Explain the purpose of this conversation.

______

______

Act 1, Scene 7: ''Twere well it were done quickly.'

In this scene, we see the complexities of the two characters.

4.11.6 Understanding and responding to texts A

1 Read Macbeth's first soliloquy and explain his argument and his conclusion.

______

______

______

______

2 Explain the metaphor in Macbeth's soliloquy, 'I have no spur to prick the sides of my intent ...'

______

______

______

3 What does the soliloquy reveal about his character?

Enter Lady Macbeth

After Macbeth's soliloquy, Shakespeare does something interesting ... **LADY MACBETH ENTERS**.

4 Discuss what you think is the purpose and effect of Lady Macbeth entering at this point in the scene.

What dramatic devices are used to construct characters?

Follow Macbeth and Lady Macbeth throughout the rest of the play. Shakespeare continues to construct and develop (but not in the self-improvement kind of way!) his characters to show how dynamic they are. We also see how their relationship is torn apart as they realise, too late, that the murder of King Duncan will have severe consequences.

Act 2, Scene 2: 'A little water cleans us of this deed'

Act 2, Scene 1: 'Is this a dagger'?

4.11.7 Understanding and responding to texts A

1 Read Macbeth's 'Is this a dagger ...' soliloquy and pay close attention to his state of mind. Identify the metaphors and allusions. Find an example of each and explain how they capture Macbeth's mental state.

2 This soliloquy allows Shakespeare to show the audience that Macbeth is still *struggling* with this decision to murder Duncan. Obviously, murdering Duncan is far more onerous than killing on the battlefield. Explain how the language features are used to construct an engaging and complex character in Macbeth.

Act 2, Scene 2: the murder

So, how are we feeling towards the Macbeths now? Do you feel sympathy for them?

Act 2, Scene 2 is key to unlocking how the audience may feel about the Macbeths. The fact that the murder of Duncan occurs offstage is significant, as it would be difficult for the audience to feel sympathetic if they were to witness the murder.

4.11.8 Understanding and responding to texts A and B

1 **What do the Macbeths say and do after the murder? Interpret what that suggests about their characters and states of mind.**

Act 3: 'Blood will have blood'

In Act 3, Shakespeare crafts a powerful series of events to demonstrate the impact of the murder of Duncan on Macbeth and his relationship with his wife.

Act 3: 'Full of scorpions is my mind'

We continue to watch how the murder is impacting Macbeth's psychological and emotional states, as well as his relationship with Lady Macbeth. Consider all that has changed in the lives of Macbeth and Lady Macbeth, beginning with the murder of Duncan. Now, after Banquo's murder, Macbeth has a secret from his wife.

4.11.9 Reading, viewing and listening to texts

Act 3, Scene 2: 'Why do you keep alone?'

In Scene 2, Lady Macbeth is alone and there's no sign of Macbeth. In fact, Lady Macbeth must *ask* for her husband. Her first comment to him is 'Why do you keep alone?' and then Macbeth reveals what he is planning to secure their position.

1 Read and/or view the scene.

2 Identify which line suggests that Lady Macbeth realises there's a fracture opening between them.

3 Macbeth and Lady Macbeth mirror each other throughout the play. Compare this scene to Act 1, Scene 7. What changes do you notice about their relationship and how decisions are being made?

4.11.10 Understanding and responding to texts A and B

Act 3, Scene 4: 'Never shake thy gory locks at me'

Here we come to the dinner party from hell.

1 Read and/or view Scene 4.

2 The ghost of Banquo appears at the banquet.

- a Discuss how the reaction of Macbeth to the ghost reveals his guilt, inner turmoil and deteriorating mental state.
- b Analyse the use of symbolism and how it suggests Macbeth's reaction. Support your answer with quotations.

Let's look at the ending of Scene 4 where Macbeth and Lady Macbeth converse. This is a sad moment in the play. They are growing apart, no longer unified and on the same path.

3 Examine Macbeth's metaphor: 'I am in blood / Stepped in so far ...' What is Macbeth revealing about himself? Write an analytical paragraph. Use quotations and examine the purpose and effect of Shakespeare's language.

Here's a starter: *At the end of Act 3, Scene 4, Shakespeare reveals to the audience an important character development in Macbeth ...*

4 How do Lady Macbeth's behaviour and speech in this scene reflect her mental and emotional state? Analyse the language choices and stage directions that reveal her transformation.

5 How does Shakespeare show Macbeth's attitude to murder in Act 3, Scene 4? Discuss.

- What is his attitude?
- How does he show it?
- Why does he have this attitude?
- How does his language reflect it?
- How does the structure of the play affect our feelings towards Macbeth?
- What message is Macbeth's attitude to murder giving us in this scene?

4.11.11 Expressing ideas and composing texts A

Lady Macbeth

Lady Macbeth's character undergoes a significant change in this scene and her role in the play diminishes after Act 3.

In your English notebook, give Lady Macbeth a chance to reveal her perspective. Compose an extra scene, a first-person narrative or soliloquy, at the end of Act 3 to give Lady Macbeth a voice and demonstrate your understanding of her character.

Act 5: a dismal and fatal end

Act 5 begins with Lady Macbeth's unconscious revelations about the murders. The audience now sees the vulnerable side of Lady Macbeth, which presents a shocking visual contrast with the Lady Macbeth of previous acts.

4.11.12 Understanding and responding to texts A and B

Lady Macbeth: 'Out, damned spot'

1 Discuss with a partner three ways that Lady Macbeth has changed from Act 1 to Act 5.

2 It's important to note here that Shakespeare highlights Lady Macbeth's isolation in Act 5, Scene 1. Explain how Shakespeare does this through language and dramatic elements, and what he is communicating here about the nature of the Macbeths' relationship at this point in the play.

____

____

____

____

3 How is the audience positioned to feel about the character of Lady Macbeth at the conclusion of the play?

____

____

____

____

4.11.13 Expressing ideas and composing texts A

Lady Macbeth's gentlewoman reports to the doctor that she writes during her sleepwalking. In your English notebook, write what you think she writes.

Macbeth: 'Throw physic to the dogs'

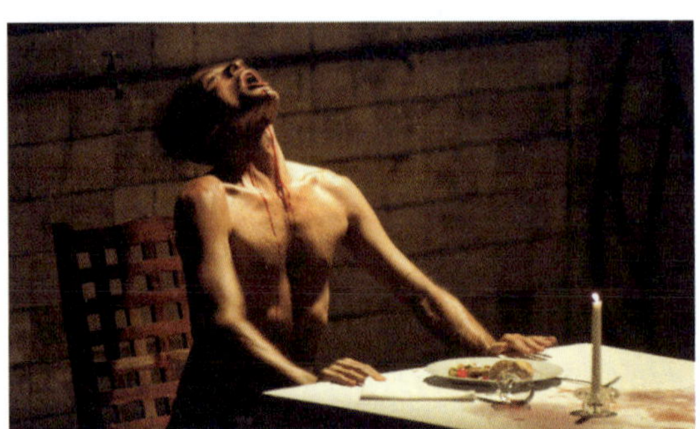

Macbeth's evil actions result, justly you might think, in his death. But are there any occasions in Act 5 when an audience might feel sympathy for him? Or even admire him? Does the audience see a side to his character that they might not have seen since Act 1?

4.11.14 Reading, viewing and listening to texts

1 Read and/or view Act 5, Scene 3.

2 Examine Macbeth's lines. Write down which words/phrases show the audience that Macbeth is:

Agitated	Regretful	Defiant

4.11.15 Expressing ideas and composing texts A

Macbeth: 'She should have died hereafter'

Consider now your impression of Macbeth. In your English notebook, rewrite Act 5, Scene 5 as a narrative, from Seyton's point of view, to show your interpretation of Macbeth's character and his reaction to the news of Lady Macbeth's death.

Extension activity

In your English notebook, write the previous scene from the perspective of both Macbeth and Seyton, using a parallel narrative structure.

4.11.16 Chapter reflection

1 Some argue that Lady Macbeth encourages her husband to be king because he is her vehicle to power. However, others argue that she's not interested in that: 'I don't think she does it for herself at all. She does it for him. She'll push him towards what she believes to be his due' (Dame Judy Dench, from *Shakespeare: The Man Who Pays the Rent*).

Reflect on your interpretation of Lady Macbeth and her motives and write a paragraph explaining what you think.

2 Let's return to the unit inquiry question: ***Does Shakespeare speak to us today?*** This chapter has encouraged you to examine how Shakespeare created engaging, dynamic and complex characters; when we analyse how he does this, we can appreciate that we have far more in common with the characters than we first realised. Outline how writing creative compositions in response to the play has enabled you to have a deeper knowledge, interpretation, analysis and appreciation of Shakespeare's characters.

CHAPTER 12: 'IF I BE WASPISH, BEST BEWARE MY STING'

Chapter overview

In this chapter, you will consider the structure and language of Shakespeare as you focus on a single play, *The Taming of the Shrew*. You will learn about the different interpretations of the play and how it can be perceived to be controversial in the twenty-first century.

You will explore the ways in which societal expectations of men and women often dictated the landscape of their relationships and how they had to dissemble to achieve their desires.

Success criteria: In this chapter, I will be successful when I can ...

- recognise how contextual expectations in society can shape relationships and provide a lens through which audiences form their interpretations
- evaluate how the authority of a text is determined by and continually reassessed by its audience
- recognise and evaluate how style can be privileged according to context
- structure a clear and convincing persuasive piece of writing.

Chapter inquiry questions

- What characterises a Shakespearean comedy?
- What is the purpose of 'the frame'?
- How does the play reflect views of relationships and marriage in the sixteenth century?
- Can you establish and sustain an interpretation using multiple sources?

Key vocabulary

- Interpretation
- Metatheatre
- Irony

What characterises a Shakespearean comedy?

The Taming of the Shrew is one of Shakespeare's comedies, believed to have been written at the end of the sixteenth century. As you might know from your study of comedy in Year 9, comedy in Shakespeare's time was different to today. Shakespearean comedy adhered to certain codes and conventions that might surprise you, but once you understand that comedy then wasn't like comedy now, his work can make a lot more sense!

4.12.1 Warm-up

'If I be waspish, best beware my sting.'

Use the quotation as inspiration for a piece of writing. Discuss as a class whether you could/should write this creatively, persuasively or discursively.

Typical conventions of a Shakespearean comedy are:

Happy endings – to be a comedy, there must be a happy ending. The resolution in Act 5 brings harmony and order to the disrupted world created earlier in the play. Forgiveness can often play a crucial role in the restoration of harmony.

Marriage as a resolution – marriage is a central theme in Shakespearean comedies and a union serves as a symbol of reconciliation. However, the journey towards marriage is often filled with misunderstandings, obstacles and comedic elements.

Mistaken identities and disguises – identities in comedies are often confused because characters disguise themselves, sometimes as a different gender or, as in *The Taming of the Shrew*, as a different class (such as a peasant for a nobleman).

Wordplay and wit – as you read, look out for clever wordplay, puns and double entendre, particularly as part of the exchange between characters, as this is often when the humour is.

Multiple storylines – tragedies such as *Macbeth* follow a single storyline, but Shakespeare's comedies invariably have multiple plots unfolding concurrently.

Satire – Shakespeare often uses the comedy of a play to lighten the atmosphere while at the same time criticising societal norms and class distinctions. Arguably, *The Taming of the Shrew* is great example of this.

4.12.2 Reading, viewing and listening to texts

As you read, keep a learning **journal** and each time you recognise one of the comedic conventions listed previously make a note of it:

- Jot down a key quotation.
- Describe the event or exchange.
- How is it designed to amuse and engage the audience?

Include writing, pictures, signs and symbols – anything that personalises your journal and deepens your understanding of the play.

Extension activity

You can broaden this activity beyond just comedy and compile your thoughts about characters and key themes as well.

You will find as you read the play that there is much, in terms of content and themes, that is not 'funny' but in fact very serious. This suggests that perhaps Shakespeare was using comedy to communicate serious ideas.

In your English notebook, you might wish to reflect on whether by using comedy to engage the audience, Shakespeare was also able to engage them in more serious concerns on the power of the sexes, which is a central theme we explore in this chapter.

This will be a great resource for you to look back on for your summative assessment task and will help you organise your thoughts and interpretations.

What is the purpose of 'the frame'?

Before you begin reading Shakespeare, it can often be helpful to know a little bit about the play, so you know the plot and don't get lost in the language.

4.12.3 Reading, viewing and listening to texts

Scan the QR code to get you started.

When you have viewed and listened to the short video, complete the activities to consolidate your knowledge.

1 What clues does the name of the play give the audience?

___

___

___

2 What is a framing device?

3 In the play the 'framing device' comes in the form of the Induction and this is when Christopher Sly – the peasant drunkard – meets the nobleman who has a sense of fun. Describe the 'frame' and the play *The Taming of the Shrew* in more detail, using the template below:

4 In the Induction, Christopher Sly speaks in prose and the nobleman in blank verse – what does this tell the audience about them?

Some performances of *The Taming of the Shrew* exclude the Induction, but it is a wonderful way to engage a theatre audience from the very beginning. The Induction is loud and bawdy, and often creates immediate comedy. However, comedy is not the only reason for the use of this framing device.

4.12.4 Expressing ideas and composing texts A

Imagine that when you wake up in the morning, you get up, go to the bathroom and look in the mirror.

What are your thoughts as you look at yourself? Do you like what you see, or do you see all your imperfections?

As you read this play, try to see the Induction as the frame and the play put on by the travelling actors, *The Taming of the Shrew*, as the mirror. As Shakespeare's contemporary audience watched the play, the attitudes and values of the characters reflected their own, similar to the way a mirror reflects you.

Remember this as you read and watch the play, as it will help you to build an interpretation of both the characters and the motivations of the playwright.

The Induction highlights the artificiality of the theatrical experience by presenting a character (Christopher Sly) who is himself a part of the audience, and yet becomes an unwitting participant in the play. This 'play within a play' structure is an example of **metatheatre**.

The framing device creates **a unified structure for the play**, tying together disparate elements and emphasising the interconnectedness of the stories. Remember there is the main plot of Katherina and Petruchio but also the sub-plots of Bianca and Lucentio and Hortensio and the widow. The frame provides a theatrical context that enhances the overall coherence of these narratives.

4.12.5 Expressing ideas and composing texts A

Choose a character from the Induction scene, such as Christopher Sly, the Lord or one of Sly's friends.

Imagine you are a journalist interviewing the chosen character. Design a set of open interview questions that delve into the character's thoughts, feelings and experiences during the events of the Induction.

Example questions:

- How did you feel about the prank played on Christopher Sly?
- What motivated you to participate in the deception?

Write the responses from the perspective of your chosen character. Alternatively, you could interview a partner and write down their responses. Do you think the Induction scene reflects any societal issues of the time?

How does the play reflect views of relationships and marriage in the sixteenth century?

A central concern of the play is relationships and marriage, and for a modern audience this is the most contentious element of *The Taming of the Shrew*. An Elizabethan audience would not have been surprised at the societal views presented, but a modern audience is rightly outraged at the misogynistic attitudes and behaviour they witness.

Your job, as a student of Shakespeare, is to decide how we might interpret Shakespeare's portrayal of this central concern today. In the sixteenth century, a woman's wedding day was one of the most important days of her life. However, there are some important differences between the reasons for marriage then and now.

In the time of Shakespeare, women of the nobility rarely married for love or had a choice in who they wedded. Marriage was usually a contractual arrangement between two families and, along with her **dowry**, on her wedding day a woman passed from the responsibility of her father to her husband.

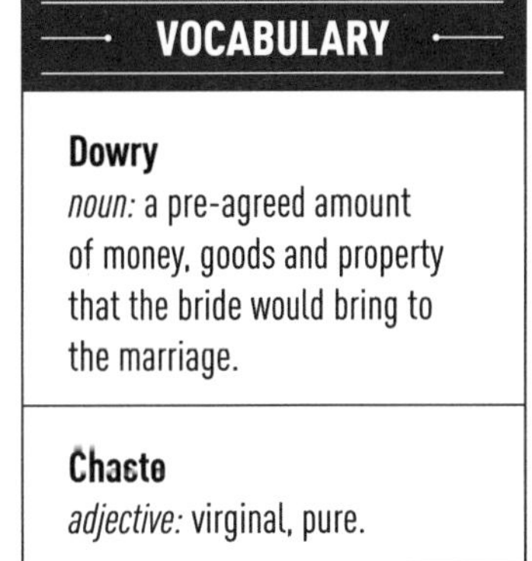
VOCABULARY

Dowry
noun: a pre-agreed amount of money, goods and property that the bride would bring to the marriage.

Chaste
adjective: virginal, pure.

Elizabethan girls were raised to be **chaste**, modest, obedient, silent and subservient to men. This was considered appropriate training for marriage. As life expectancy was low, birth control nonexistent and child mortality high, young women usually married in their teens and were expected to have as many children as they could. Women were not allowed to own property, and any inherited income they had was transferred to their husband on marriage.

Men were seen as protectors of women, and arguably of the patriarchal society they were part of and perpetuated. They were expected to be physically strong, virile and dominant in a marriage and were usually more educated than women.

Scan the QR code for additional activities.

Can you establish and sustain an interpretation using multiple sources?

As you will know from your reading of *The Taming of the Shrew*, there is no doubt that Petruchio's behaviour towards Katherina is violent, domineering and completely unacceptable. However, at the time of Shakespeare this behaviour was at worst commonplace and at best expected.

In Elizabethan times, to have a 'shrewish' wife reflected badly on the husband; onlookers saw him as weak and unable to control her. To be considered a 'shrewish' woman meant that it was difficult to find suitors and so you were destined to be a spinster. Remember how Baptista determines that Katherina's more popular younger sister, Bianca, cannot marry until Katherina herself has?

Some critics have dismissed the play as misogynistic and without a place in a modern age. However, arguably, Katherina and Petruchio are both seeking a happy and fruitful marriage, in which they don't have to be cowed by another. They are both strong-willed and their wordplay indicates sharp minds and tongues.

At the end of Act 5 Katherina's closing monologue would suggest that she has been 'tamed' by Petruchio – read an extract of her lines below where it seems as though she is describing an earlier version of herself:

> **A woman moved is like a fountain troubled,**
> **Muddy, ill-seeming, thick, bereft of beauty;**
> **And while it is so, none so dry or thirsty**
> **Will deign to sip or touch one drop of it.**

4.12.6 Understanding and responding to texts A

1 What do you understand by the simile used in lines 1 and 2? What is Katherina saying about women here?

---

2 In lines 3 and 4 Katherina states the consequences of 'a woman moved'. What are they?

---

3 How has Katherina's opinion changed from Act 1? Explain your thinking.

I am ashamed that women are so simple
To offer war where they should kneel for peace;
Or seek for rule, supremacy and sway,
When they are bound to serve, love and obey.

4 Discuss with a partner: What might a modern audience object to here?

My mind hath been as big as one of yours,
My heart as great, my reason haply more,
To bandy word for word and frown for frown;
But now I see our lances are but straws,
Our strength as weak, our weakness past compare,
That seeming to be most which we indeed least are.
Then vail your stomachs, for it is no boot,
And place your hands below your husband's foot:
In token of which duty, if he please,
My hand is ready; may it do him ease.

5 Read this extract aloud with a partner. Together change it to a more contemporary style of English.

6 When you are happy with your modern version, write it below.

7 With a partner or in a small group, compare Katherina's final speech with one of your choice earlier in the play – perhaps from Act 2, Scene 1 when she is verbally sparring with Petruchio.

- You might wish to compare changes in character or how Katherina's language has mellowed from the beginning to the end of the play.
- Compare her final speech with one of Petruchio's where he lets the audience knows what he desires in a wife to show whether he got it.

Brainstorm all your ideas in the space below and then choose ONE idea to craft a comparative paragraph with a clear topic sentence, comparative vocabulary and supporting evidence.

(If you are working in a small group you might wish to each take a different idea. Your teacher may task you with writing a collaborative essay.)

4.12.7 Expressing ideas and composing texts A

Extended writing

Your goal: To show critical thinking skills and an ability to synthesise information from multiple texts to create an interpretation by:

- drawing on prior knowledge of the play to inform your understanding
- questioning, challenging and deepening your understanding of new and familiar texts
- discerning the reliability of source material
- researching, selecting and sequencing appropriate evidence to construct cohesive and authoritative arguments.

Your task: Individually or with a partner (under the direction of your teacher):

- Research three different critical interpretations of *The Taming of the Shrew* where the central concern is gender, relationships and marriage.
- Create a multi-modal presentation which explores each of the interpretations offered.
- Evaluate each one – do you agree or disagree, and why?
- Formulate your own interpretation based on your findings and knowledge of the play.
- Design an essay question that would use your research and create your thesis statement based on your own interpretation.

[TIP: Avoid course help guides. Try a platform such as Google Scholar to get you started.]

4.12.8 Chapter reflection

1 Your teacher has asked you whether you think this play is worth teaching the following year – what would you say?

Think about what you have learned: not just about the play, but about interpretation, researching and forming an argument from different sources.

2 Many of Shakespeare's female characters challenge societal expectations and traditional roles. Are the characters in this play different? Reflecting on your study of this play, do you think that Shakespeare is condoning coercive control in marriage or spotlighting it to challenge us?

3 Let's reflect on the unit inquiry question: ***Does Shakespeare speak to us today?*** Consider *The Taming of the Shrew* in the light of this question and sum up your response in no more than 100 words.

Unit 4: **Summative assessment**

The summative assessment options below provide opportunities to demonstrate your achievement of the following outcomes and focus areas.

Outcome and focus area	**EN5-RVL-01** **Reading, viewing and listening to texts**	**EN5-URA-01** **Understanding and responding to texts A**	**EN5-URB-01** **Understanding and responding to texts B**	**EN5-ECA-01** **Expressing ideas and composing texts A**	**EN5-ECB-01** **Expressing ideas and composing texts B**
Content point	Reflecting	Characterisation	Theme Perspective and context Argument and authority Style	Speaking Text features Word-level language	Planning, monitoring and revising

Option 1: The poet's pen creates the shapes

Consider the influence of Shakespeare's language on contemporary literature, film and television. Modern writers adapt or draw inspiration from his linguistic style to speak to contemporary audiences.

In what ways does Shakespeare's inventive vocabulary and wordplay not only enrich the language of his time but also continue to influence and shape the evolution of the English language today?

Create and record a podcast in which you evaluate this question. Refer to a variety of Shakespeare's plays and poetry, and other texts of your own choosing, to illustrate your viewpoint and persuade your audience.

Be guided by the following questions when planning, writing and producing your composition.

- Which Shakespeare plays and poetry, and modern sources, will I use to show how the English language is influenced and shaped by Shakespeare?
- What is my thesis?
- Who is my audience?

Option 2: Shattered ambitions –*Macbeth*

The unit inquiry question asks you to evaluate whether Shakespeare speaks to us today.

How does a contemporary adaptation or transformation of *Macbeth* sustain interest in the characters and values of the play?

Consider this question in light of your study of the play and create and present a multimodal presentation.

You may answer this question by referring to one scene from *Macbeth* or an entire act, and one other transformation of *Macbeth*.

Research a film adaptation or transformation of *Macbeth*. Choose one that you think best engages a contemporary audience through its representation of Macbeth, Lady Macbeth and their relationship, and compare it with the play. Some suggested film versions are those starring Michael Fassbender, Orson Welles, Patrick Stewart, and Ian McKellen.

Be guided by the following questions when planning, writing and producing your composition.

- Which scene or act and modern adaptation/transformation will I use?
- What is my thesis?
- Who is my audience?
- How can I use reviews and academic articles to help me construct my argument?
- How does the film adaptation/transformation represent Macbeth and Lady Macbeth? Does that align with my interpretation?
- How does the film enable audiences to negotiate and reassess representations of Macbeth, Lady Macbeth and their relationship?

Option 3: 'If I be waspish, best beware my sting' – *The Taming of the Shrew*

This unit invites you to consider the gender politics of this Shakespeare play. You have considered the context, events, characters and language of the play in addition to different interpretations of this play.

For this task you are going to write the argument to use in a class debate, in which the motion is:

The *Taming of the Shrew* is a play in which Shakespeare is condoning coercive control in marriage and thus has no place in a modern theatre.

Your teacher will tell you whether you are to create an argument for or against this motion. As you prepare your case, work in a small group to share knowledge and ideas.

As you prepare, remember to:

- use the play as your primary source
- research a variety of different interpretations of the play – both in support of your argument and against so you are ready to counter your opponents!

Ensure that your argument has clarity and authority created by both your evidence and the way that you express it.

Now – use your skills of persuasion to turn your written ideas into a spoken debate!

Assessment as learning: self-assessment

Does my composition:

- [ ] research, select and sequence evidence from Shakespeare's plays and reliable sources to construct cohesive and authoritative arguments?
- [ ] evaluate how the authority of Shakespeare's plays is continually negotiated and reassessed by readers?
- [ ] develop an effective thesis?
- [ ] use the structural conventions of persuasive texts to justify opinions and develop arguments?
- [ ] introduce and define complex key ideas, academic concepts and positions for arguments?
- [ ] use purposeful verbal and/or nonverbal language to emphasise key points, enhance engagement and clarify meaning?
- [ ] include use of intonation, emphasis, volume, pace and timing (where appropriate)?
- [ ] signal the development of ideas through language, structure and presentational features?

How effectively did my plan and drafts help me to draft and revise my composition?

____

____

____

What are two strengths of my response?

____

____

What area/s of my response do I need to refine further?

____

____

ACKNOWLEDGEMENTS

Insight Publications thanks the authors, Emma Wynne-Jones and Bronwyn Ralphs, for their work on *English for NSW, Year 10, Stage 5*.

Insight Publications is also grateful to the following individuals and organisations for permission to reproduce copyright material.

Texts: English K–10 Syllabus © NSW Education Standards Authority for and on behalf of the Crown in right of the State of New South Wales, 2012; Excerpts from *Lark* by Anthony McGowan, Copyright © Anthony McGowan; Excerpts from *Catching Teller Crow* by Ambelin Kwaymullina and Ezekiel Kwaymullina, Copyright © Ambelin Kwaymullina and Ezekiel Kwaymullina; Excerpts from *The Catcher in the Rye* by J.D. Salinger (Copyright © 1945, 1946, 1951 by J.D. Salinger, © renewed 1973, 1974, 1979 by J.D. Salinger) appear courtesy of the J.D. Salinger Literary Trust; The Project Gutenberg eBook of *A Study In Scarlet*, by Arthur Conan Doyle; Billy Collins, 'Embrace' from *The Apple That Astonished Paris*, Copyright © 1988, 1996 by Billy Collins. Reprinted with the permission of The Permissions Company, LLC on behalf of the University of Arkansas Press, uapress.com; Billy Collins, 'The Country' from *Nine Horses*, reprinted with permission of Pan Macmillan; Billy Collins, excerpt from 'Schoolsville' from *The Apple That Astonished Paris*, Copyright © 1988, 1996 by Billy Collins, reprinted with the permission of The Permissions Company, LLC on behalf of the University of Arkansas Press, uapress.com; '[i carry your heart with me(i carry it in]'. Copyright 1952, © 1980, 1991 by the Trustees for the E. E.Cummings Trust, from *Complete Poems*: 1904–1962 by E. E. Cummings, edited by George J. Firmage, used by permission of Liveright Publishing Corporation.

Images: *Catching Teller Crow* cover © Ambelin Kwaymullina and Ezekiel Kwaymullina; Tom Richmond, Richmond Illustration Inc.http://www.tomrichmond.com; tom@tomrichmond.com; *Stardust* cover by Nail Gaiman and Charles Vess, DCPress@dcentertainment.com; *Stardust* cover by Nail Gaiman and Charles Vess, Headline Publishing Group Limited. The following images from Alamy: *The Catcher in the Rye*, Ben Stiller *Zoolander*; Studio publicity still from *National Lampoon's Vacation* Christie Brinkley © 1983 Warner All Rights Reserved; Hanse; *Stardust* film poster; Sherlock Holmes; *The Slave Ship* by J. M. W. Turner; *Wanderer above the Sea of Fog* by Caspar David Friedrich; Macbeth with dagger; Lady Macbeth; Macbeth anguish.